THINKING ABOUT TEACHING

A RURAL SOCIAL STUDIES TEACHER'S PATH TO STRIVE FOR RELEVANCE

CASEY JAKUBOWSKI

Published by EduMatch®
PO Box 150324, Alexandria, VA 22315
www.edumatchpublishing.com

These books are available at special discounts when purchased in quantities of 10 or more for use as premiums, promotions fundraising, and educational use. For inquiries and details, contact the publisher: sarah@edumatch.org.

Names are changed to protect the innocent, and people with very good lawyers!

ISBN: 978-1-970133-22-6

CONTENTS

PART III
RURAL EDUCATION

PART IV
THE CONCLUSION

INTRODUCTION

Welcome to a practical book I wrote to share with you, the readers, concerning some tips, tricks, and musings after 20 years in the profession. The journey we take together, you in a hopefully cozy environment, and me, down the past of memory lane, is collaborative, and engaging. I WANT you to mark up this book! I want you to underline, highlight, make notes, and write messages in the margins. I want you, reader, to enter into a partnership, and make education better for everyone. You, reader, are the most important person in a child's life right now, and I want this dialogue to engage you, to inspire you, and to grab you. Our journey through the educational realities of the present-day can only make life so much better!

I am on social media, and you can direct message me on

Twitter (@CaseyJ_edu)! Let's engage in creating a better today throughout the book!

I hope what follows can help on their journey, be it at the beginning in a methods class, in the first years of their darkest nights teaching, or mid-career and later. For the next few chapters in the book, I want you to join me on a journey of memory and reflection on how educators can take everyday occurrences and reflect on how to plan really great lessons and powerful activities to keep the day to day of class inspired.

1. TEA, COFFEE, OR COCOA?

I have been thinking a lot about education. Academics and extracurricular activities are in full swing. As I write this, I am thinking about my friends and students who are in the middle of studying, writing, or correcting papers. This is the time of the year that reality has set in. The syllabus tells us the first assignments of the term are due. For many students in K-12, the first unit test is right around the corner.

All of these facts can induce anxiety for everyone involved. For the students, they may ask themselves: did I study enough for the test? Were the notes I took in the class enough to help me? Did I do the readings? Our students often struggle with the necessary study and organizational skills. In many families, organization and organizing are difficult for adults as well as students. Many self-help books have been published on how to declutter one's life. Organization classes are standard offerings in community education sessions for adults. In schools, some freshman year classes in high school are designed to help students become more organized in their coursework.

For teachers, the anxiety comes from ensuring their students do well and that the scores improve. Teachers also want to help their own families and make sure their own children are doing well. Anxiety over how their students do, how their colleagues are doing, and how their community will do are all part of the teacher's day. Educators tend to worry. Teaching is a profession which is a vocation, not just a job. Anxiety within the profession has been exacerbated by society, demanding that educators do more. Many self-help books tell people to shut out the external chatter, and believe in yourself —but what do you do when it's not you, but your profession that people are questioning and repeatedly demanding to do better?

For parents, the anxiety originates with their desire to see their children have a leg up on life. Parents want to know how well their kids fit in at school, if their friends are a good influence, and if they are following a path that is conducive to success. Parents want to know the taxes invested in the school are producing educated children who can gain entry into a good college. Parents want a good neighborhood where their children are safe. Parents also want to make sure the teachers are doing a good job teaching their students as individuals and not as numbers.

On one episode of *The Big Bang Theory* (Warner Brothers Entertainment), Sheldon Cooper's mother advises him to offer tea to distressed guests. Other people may offer coffee or cocoa to people when they need to talk and have a conversation. While it might be helpful to provide people with a hot beverage to help soothe their minds, we need to provide something more substantial: our support.

Our levels of support can mirror the three levels of drinks: t*ea level* support would include a basic level of support that has healthy qualities. Tea is easy to make: drop a bag into boiling water and let it steep. Tea level support is when people can say very quickly, "How are you, how is it going?" Every educator should offer our students, parents, teachers, and friends a "tea" level of support at a minimum every day. It is easy, and it is quick.

The *coffee level* of support takes more effort. Coffee requires using beans to make coffee and has caffeine. Therefore, it is essential for many people. Coffee level support is going beyond the basic "tea level" to offer a person a healthy and supportive outlet for what ails them.

Coffee level support may require a lightener and a sweetener. Sometimes, it's important to help lighten the load for our students and colleagues. We may occasionally also need to sweeten the bitterness. Coffee support includes allowing a person to truly offer substantial support when others are having difficulty.

Cocoa support is the most involved level of support. A mug of cocoa is offered when one wants comfort. There is hot water, chocolate, sugar, whipped cream, and marshmallows. It can include a sprinkle of cocoa on top and is extremely complicated to make. Cocoa level of support is given only in the most complicated cases, such as offering support to our anxious friends, students, colleagues, and parents. But to many teachers, the cocoa level of support is a daily event. Students, especially those living in poverty, often need multiple cups of cocoa every day from their teachers.

In the *Harry Potter* (Rowling, 2002) series, chocolate is one of the cures when a Dementor attacks a person. A Dementor is an evil creature that pulls the very living soul out of a person. To our students, poverty, violence, hunger, drugs, and family instability are the Dementors. The teachers are the chocolate providers.

———

Think of the last time you gave support to a colleague. What did you do, and what level of support did you provide? Tweet about it to **#ThinkingAboutTeachingBook**

PART I

REFLECTING ON EDUCATION AND THE ART OF TEACHING

In this section, I look back at developing as a teacher, and my journey through the classroom, from a novice educator to a more experienced practitioner. I make an attempt to describe my journey in the hopes that novice, mid-career, and experienced practitioners can laugh (a lot), learn or be reminded of something, and, most importantly, realize we are all in this together—as a community.

Teaching is an individual act within a team approach. Just as a musician is responsible for their own part in an orchestra, a teacher is part of a much larger collective. With one violin playing, a beautiful sound emerges to thrill the audience. When the whole orchestra plays, people can be moved to tears. One teacher can make a difference in a child's life, but the profession can change the world.

Please enjoy this section, and by all means, take notes in the margins, highlight, copy (please follow fair copyright laws!) and use what is contained within to help your journey.

2. BUILDING TIES WITH STUDENTS

*S*tudent success in school depends on relationships. Research on at-risk learners is evident: an adult who takes an interest in helping a student increases their opportunity to graduate. (McDaniel & Yarbrough, 2016). But it is not teachers alone who must take an active role in a student's life. Every member of the school community needs to help students become successful.

A school that has developed a sound and robust example of relationships between all members of the community and students is the Rochester, NY International Academy (RIA). Rochester is the third-largest city in New York State, and faces several issues with poverty, racial inequality, and urban blight. Designed as the first school for refugee students to the United States, RIA has developed a standard among the entire community within the school for relationships. This characterization starts at the top with the principal, Mary Diaz. She leads the school by example. Her daily routine includes greeting students as they arrive on campus and saying hello to fellow staff members during the day as walkarounds happen to each classroom, the gym, and the cafeteria. Mary and her staff ensure that students are greeted with warm smiles and have people to care and talk to throughout their day. An urban school, RIA provides a safe place for students as they transition from their war-torn homelands to the United States.

Another school that does relationships right is Wellsville, NY Central School District. This rural community near Pennsylvania helps students see success beyond the school system. The region is most known for its mountains and outdoor recreational opportunities. The school has developed a college and career mindset and ensures that all students have someone they can turn to during their searches for colleges or careers. It is a place with technology, innovation, and an unwavering demand for excellence. The superintendent at Wellsville, Kim Muller, sets the expectation that all students will be successful, and helps her administrative, teaching, and support staff see that in every child. For a smaller, rural community, Wellsville has a lot to offer its students and their families in terms of building relationships. At school, the students know they have resources in teachers, principals, and support staff.

In Watervliet, a small city in New York State's capital region, fourth-grade teacher Mrs. Kathy Grill works closely with her students, reading to them every day after lunch. Her students love her attention to detail, her suggestions for books, and working with their classmates—all because she reads to them. Kathy also volunteers at the public library for her district. She provides a friendly and smiling face for students who are living in deep poverty and a transient environment. Kathy aims to be a stable and constant force for her students.

As a former member of the New York State Education Department's Office of School Improvement, I would visit schools that were often under review for poor academic performance. What was evident on many visits were the broken relationships between the district officials with the students, teachers, administrators, and parents. The school district leadership had created an environment that did not support student engagement and learning. One of the first recommendations the review team often made involved developing better relationships between the district officials and the students, teachers, administrators, and parents. A resource that many teachers consult is Wong and Wong's work *The First Days of School (2009)*, which offers many tips and tricks to build a relationship that supports student engagement and academic achievement. A simple one, greeting a student by his/her name, is easy and critical for success.

Here I include an experience I had as a teacher in rural New York State. Brand new to the district of 200 students and fresh out of college, I was assigned a senior economics class. One of my students, the youngest member of his family and a basic training graduate, did not like school. He had come that year, ready to graduate and to serve in the Army. Early in October, a disagreement between this student and the principal developed, and the young man dropped out of school.

Later that week, I saw him in the only fast food place in town. I sat down at his table, and we talked for five minutes. When I left him, I asked for the school's economics book back, and I joked the district would make me pay for it if he didn't return it. About two weeks later, he re-enrolled in school and graduated in June. When I finally did get his book back, he wrote me a small note: "Mr. J., Hey here is your book back. Thanks for asking for it. I came back to give it to you."

If I had not asked for the book back, would this young man have come back to school? I hate to think of the alternative.

One of the Common Core State Standards focuses on persuasive writing. Students can identify and write a letter to any adult who has helped make a difference in their lives. The person can be school-based, community-based, or someone who has inspired their lives through a speech, a book, or a video. Get students to say thanks—have the students write about how much that individual helped them achieve better.

———

What are your best tips for building relationships with students?

Tweet them to **#ThinkingAboutTeachingBook**

3. THE LEADERSHIP OF OPTIMUS PRIME

*A*s a kid growing up, the Transformers (Fast & Örnebring, 2017) were one of my favorite TV shows. I enjoyed the excitement in the cartoon, and more importantly, the toys! If I were a gamer, I would appreciate the Autobots—the good guys as part of the "Chaotic Good" realm. The Autobots, from another planet, left their world to find and hunt down the evil Decepticons. The ship carrying both robots crash-landed on earth during the Age of the Dinos. When an earthquake millions of years later awoke the bots, their computer scanned the surrounding world and had the bots transform from robots into different types of vehicles. The Autobots were composed mostly of ground vehicle robots, such as tanks, ambulances, trucks, cars, and 18-wheelers, and were led by their "Prime," Optimus Prime. His leadership style embodied what Greenleaf called Servant Leadership.

THE NAME ITSELF OPTIMUS PRIME IS LATINESQUE—OPTIMUS meaning "best" or "great" and prime meaning "first." The leader was the first best. Originally, Optimus started as Orion Pax, which has Greek roots of "Heaven's Light" and Peace. So really, Optimus is a peaceful leader who is the best. The character really lives up to the name in the show and the cartoon. The Autobot commander, while authoritative, cares very deeply for his followers. He ensures he leads with their best interests in mind. He does not like violence but will use it in pursuit of a peaceful goal.

Optimus also believes deeply in the opinions of his followers. Before embarking on events, projects, or decisions, he seeks their input. He asks for advice from both his experienced and newest team members, as well as from outsiders, including, in the cartoon's instance, humans. Often, he asks the opinion of everyone before making a decision. This is critical in a servant leader, for they seek input from all members of their team, weighing all of the facts before making a decision.

When a decision is to be made, the leader takes full responsibility. Quite often, Optimus would tell his followers that he had to do something, or he was responsible for the decision. This burden weighed on the character's shoulders heavily. Sometimes we would see him in contemplation away and alone from his team, where he wondered about his actions and their impacts. Optimus would lead from the front in the battles against the Decepticons. He was first on the road, first to transform, and with his team out in front. The character led from the front and was with the team in the heat of the action at all times.

Sacrifice also comes to mind when discussing Prime. In *Transformers the Movie*, Optimus Prime makes the ultimate sacrifice and is killed. For a nine-year-old kid, this was a huge, emotional, and overwhelming moment! Prime sacrifices his own well-being to ensure the survival of his team and his followers. So many times, in so many series, the character of Optimus Prime places the needs of others ahead of his own. Philosophically speaking, it is very much like the Utilitarianism of John Stuart Mill. In this philosophy, the greatest good for the greatest number should drive decision-making.

The Prime gave some important life lessons in leadership to young kids watching that cartoon in the 1980s. I was one of them.

Outside of the education world itself, where do you draw inspiration for teaching?
Tweet about it using **#ThinkingAboutTeachingBook**

4. BEST LESSON I EVER DID

*I*t's been a few decades since I started teaching in 1998. That is 2/3rds of a career for some people in education. Every once in a while, when my mind drifts, or I can't sleep at night, memories both good and bad come back to haunt me. Then I get my brain revving to try and figure out what I could have done differently or better. Today, while walking in amazingly beautiful upstate New York, I was pondering the best lesson I ever taught.

In this age of accountability and teacher evaluation, the idea of a "best lesson" is not discussed—instead it's "did this lesson meet the standards of _____ teacher evaluation rubric?" Danielson, the New York State United Teacher's (NYSUT) model, and others all discuss the impact of a lesson through measurement and evaluation. I am going to dwell on Danielson because that is what I taught through when at

Sidney, NY, a small rural upstate community in New York State, and was trained to evaluate while at Rochester as the Social Studies Director. The first Domain of Danielson's rubric is *Planning and Preparation*. The domain is divided into two subparts: *Content & Pedagogy* and *Designing Coherent Strategy*. This section wants to help teachers get better at how they teach, what they teach, and in what order they teach. It serves as a guide for best practices for teachers and others to look at planning, instruction, and delivery in the classroom. The goal of the framework is to assist teachers in engaging with the profession from a model of strength.

The second domain is the classroom environment, and it too is divided into two parts: *creating an environment of respect and rapport*, as well as the second part of *managing student behavior*. The goal of this section of the framework is to get teachers to think about how the classroom is structured. Teachers are asked to ensure that the learning environment is supportive, positive, and creative. Teachers are also asked to clearly state how they manage student behaviors in the classroom and how they ensure that behavioral issues do not interfere with learning.

The third domain is *instruction*. Here, three subparts are identified: *questioning/ discussion techniques*, *engaging students in learning*, and *using assessment to monitor progress*. The third domain is the implementation of how teachers actually teach in their classrooms. It asks teachers to lay out explicitly how they will get students to learn materials.

The domain suggests that teachers have to use a wide variety of techniques to invigorate student learning. Teachers need to make sure that students are active learners and are understanding and retaining information. This domain also asks teachers how they plan to make sure students have learned and can demonstrate that learning in a variety of formats.

The fourth domain is *professional growth and development*. This area asks teachers to reflect on how well they have started as a professional, what has been done to help them grow, and how that growth is evident. Is the learning getting better? Do students have a better grasp of knowledge?

Let's think about that for a minute. Here are some guiding questions:

1. Do you know your stuff?
2. Can you teach it well?
3. Do students and you know how to get from September to June in an organized way?
4. Is the classroom safe, orderly, and helpful?
5. Are the students working on-task and with each other?
6. Can you and your students discuss and verbally interact with materials and each other?
7. Do the students look bored?
8. How do you and the student know they have learned something?

These eight fundamental questions sum up the framework. So, let's use the best lesson I ever taught as a case study: Foods in the Columbian Exchange.

Background

In order to have earned professional certification in New York State back in the day (the early 2000s), a teacher needed to film the class and themselves teaching. They then paid a boatload of money to some company to get the tapes evaluated to show the state that they were good enough to teach. Since then, things have changed, and teachers now are never permanently certified. They must engage in Continuing Teacher and Leader Education (CTLE) professional development and pay fees every time the certification comes up for renewal.

For my best lesson, I planned a lesson that I thought was amazing! My Global History and Geography class (sophomores) were in the Renaissance and Reformation unit that would ready them for the Global History and Geography (GHG) exam. The GHG exam is an end of course exam which covers all of human history. The class actually covers two years (ninth and tenth grades). Students in the course sit for a three-hour exam where they need to answer 50 multiple choice questions, write a thematic essay based on an item from the 10 themes of social studies, answer 10-13 short answer document questions, and then write an essay based on documents and outside information. This usually takes place in a large gym in

New York in June (hot and humid—no A/C). The Renaissance and Reformation unit included some discussion on the Age of Exploration.

The Columbian Exchange is the massive diffusion of animals, plants, microbes, and technology between the Eastern and Western Hemisphere. Part of the Renaissance and Reformation revolved around power—the Age of Exploration focused on power: religious, economic, and political. Alfred Crosby (2003) wrote a great book about it. I planned the following lesson:

1. Gathering and introduction: What was the Columbian Exchange? (Five-minute mini-lesson on the Exchange)
2. Description of the activity: Students are placed into teams of four to five each. They are then given a worksheet that contains three columns. The students are to identify different foods, the taste of the foods, and how those foods may be used in the culture of the home area and the new area.
3. Rice-Corn-Wheat
4. Mango-Oranges-Strawberries
5. Cinnamon-Chili Powder-Horseradish
6. Students research using textbooks and documents provided regarding some of the technologies and diseases exchanged.

7. What was the impact on each hemisphere from technology exchanges?
8. Using the chart from *Guns, Germs, and Steel* (Diamond, 1998), describe how the Europeans used technology to their advantage in Imperialism.
9. Discuss how Native Americans utilized and adopted technology.

I also took my idea and made it into a Center for Teaching American History project at Binghamton University (http://ctah.binghamton.edu/student/jaku/caseyprint.html).

I think the lesson went great—the students tried a wide variety of fruits and grains and spices! Some remembered this experience and wrote about it on the Regents exam. My colleagues were not impressed and thought I spent way too much money on the stuff for class. (It was like $75 — three sections with 25 kids in each section). But was it a great lesson? Did I meet the domains from Mrs. Danielson's rubric?

DOMAIN 1:

Content & Pedagogy: So, I knew my stuff — after all, I was a Fredonia State Outstanding history major! I read *Guns, Germs, and Steel* (Diamond, 1998), and Crosby's (2003) book on the Columbian Exchange! Pedagogy: I wanted to create a station-based learning activity that required students to investigate foods and documents that were part of the exchange.

They then had to do some research and fill out a document that captured their findings. Okay, not bad. I could have gone deeper—made them present and question each other, or write a letter or essay about the topic. Nowadays I could ask the students to do some really technologically advanced things, like podcasts.

Coherent instruction: Yeah, well—therein lies the issue...not too coherent. Students are great, in that they will tell you if you missed something. "I don't understand" only begins to describe my afternoon classes. My morning classes were great—they totally knew what to do, and were totally the A performers in the school. The video evidence, however, shows them throwing food at each other. Yikes. Apparently, my written directions and my verbal directions were too succinct (cough, cough, whoops!), and global in nature. No concrete examples, no milestones of what to expect next, no time checks. I did walk around the room, but that didn't really help—until they saw how other students completed the activity. Thank goodness for peer-driven learning.

DOMAIN 2:

Creating an environment of respect and rapport. In teenagers? Are you kidding me? Oh...I'm an adult—sorry. I showed the students respect; they, however, were not quite into helping me out. For many, teenage rebellion had struck, and the idea of listening to a 20-something-year-old overweight kid who was scholarly and from outside of the area wasn't high on their radar. I tried—we had rules...oh well.

Managing student behavior: Mostly good, except for the thrown fruit. By the way, if you ever learn how to see with eyes in the back of your head, please let me know. The camera caught many examples of positive and not-so-positive behavior.

DOMAIN 3:

Questioning/discussion techniques: I thought they were okay questions...describe, evaluate, rank, discuss. Not bad, could have gone deeper: what parallels can you draw with other exchanges, such as technology? How did European Imperialism affect Africa? To what extent did China adapt to European Imperialism?

Engaging students in learning: many were engaged — they liked the foods. Researching, not so much. Many of the groups were still confused about the overall lesson objective. Now, the national or C3 Social Studies standards (NCSS, 2014) calls it the "Enduring Question." I wished I would have made that part more explicit (writing it on the board and the handout, which goes to pedagogy and planning coherent instruction).

Using assessment to monitor progress: I monitored and observed. I collected the document research sheet. I put the exact drawing used in the activity from Diamond's (1998) *Guns, Germs, and Steel* on the unit test, but I forgot the entrance and exit ticket. (Entrance tickets: What do the students already know about the day? Exit ticket: What did they learn, and what do they still want to learn about?) The Know- Want to Know- Learned (KWL) Chart is one of the greatest inventions in education—and we really don't, in my opinion, use it enough. It really gives students the ability to self-assess where they are, map out experiences for the unit, and evaluate what was learned and what gaps they still have.

I TAUGHT THIS LESSON IN 2002 OR 2003. I CAN'T QUITE remember. After almost 15 additional years of reflection, I really would have given myself a "Developing" rating. When I was my 2002-3 self, I thought I was "Proficient." Along the scale of the rubric, the worst is "Ineffective." This is reserved for disasters in the classroom. The next step, "Developing," means there is a spark, a good thought—yet not quite there yet. The next on the scale is "Effective," meaning good job, you did it well. Some areas need improvement, but no central critical parts are missing. The top, or "Proficient," is reserved for superstars who blow people's minds away. Proficient teachers are fantastic.

Without a doubt, I am so glad I did well enough with the First Period to earn a passing score and permanent certification. My best wasn't good enough then, so now, as I teach college, I really think through my lessons, consult with others, and ask for help. Back then, I was too scared that people would have seen me as incompetent. In reality, the most competent know what they don't know and ask for help from more experienced or knowledgeable sources. So, this is a bit of an apology to my 10th graders for a "C" level lesson back then. Hopefully, the teaching deities can forgive me too.

What was your <u>best lesson ever</u>?
Tweet about it using **#ThinkingAboutTeachingBook**

5. WORST LESSON EVER

*A*s of September 2018, I have officially hit mid-career. After graduating from the Teaching Social Studies 7-12 Bachelors of Arts program at SUNY Fredonia's School of Education, I entered my first job at a rural school district of 240 K-12 kids that no longer exists near the Pennsylvania border with New York. Growing up in suburban Hamburg, near Buffalo, I was used to a graduating class that size. Now, I would be working with social studies students in the seventh, ninth, eleventh, and twelfth grades. Yikes. We were also on a block schedule as well, so this was really new to me. Blocking was never covered in college, so I had to learn on the fly. I was also teaching four different preparations, which in many suburban and urban districts would be against the contract! But in rural schools, you do what you have to do to survive.

So, the worst lesson I ever taught was in the days before the teacher evaluation rubrics. Lessons were evaluated by whatever instrument the school administrator and the union determined would be a good fit. In my school, it was very narrative, so it was a time/action running record of what happened in the class. So, let's begin the reflection into a horrible lesson.

We had learned Madeline Hunter's (1985) model of lesson planning in undergrad: pre-opening, opening, body, review, conclusion, assessment. This is a very structured form of a lesson plan, and for a new teacher, it's especially useful for keeping you on track, except for one little problem. By February, I was overwhelmed with teaching four preps and six classes each day. It was too much. I wasn't really lesson planning so much as identifying resources and listing them in the lesson plan sheet the district gave to us. Tired does not begin to describe the exhaustion I was feeling.

Additionally, I had no mentor, as mine was out on medical leave, and many other teachers weren't as forthcoming as they could have been (or I didn't know they were offering help). I thought I was doing fine; after all, I was a member of the education honors society Kappa Delta Pi and had graduated with Honors in Liberal Education and *Summa Cum Laude* honors on my degree. Arrogance and pride before the fall, I guess...

So, that mid-winter day, I showed two videos in my 72-minute block class to ninth graders in the Global Studies I class. These students were Regents track students who would need to take an end of course exam next year while they were 10th graders. They would face 48 multiple-choice questions and three essays about the enduring themes of Global History. In our small district, every student was a Regents track student. Your section, though, was determined by when you attended Career and Technical Education at the local Board of Cooperative Education Services. Usually, the AM section was for the top kids in the school, and the PM section were kids who were not drawn to academic pursuits.

I cannot even remember what those two videos were on. I had given directions verbally to my students to "take notes as you watch the video." That was it. I popped the video in and let it play. Occasionally, I'd stop the video, or make a comment about what the program was talking about, but that was it.

"Train wreck" would be way too polite to describe how bad it was. So, let's go through what I did wrong:

1. I did not plan. What was my goal for the day? How did this lesson advance the students' knowledge about the content and skills of a historian? How was this aligned with the expectations for students to be successful at the end of the course exam?
2. I did not know my class well. First, they did not have the skills to "take notes" on a video, as I had never cognitively coached them on the process. I never introduced how I wanted the students to take

notes from lectures/lessons in class. I never gave
them leading questions to make sure they were
cued into the important stuff. Worst of all, I forgot
Learning 101: attention span. Most students have a
15-minute attention span, but I had them watch 70
minutes of a pretty dull social studies history
video.

3. There was no accountability for learning. I did not
   see how they learned, what they learned, or what
   was so significant about their learning. There is a
   ton of research (Aidinopoulou & Sampson, 2017;
   Fisher, 2018) which indicates students need
   structure to help ensure that they are learning, and
   this was really passive.

So, if I had to do it again, I would have:

1. Clearly articulated my goals: which C3 and NYS
   standards does the lesson align with? Which part of
   the CCLS aligned Framework does this lesson
   tie to?
2. Knowledge activation: What do you already know,
   and what do you want to know about the subject?
3. Different stations for learning:
4. The first station: a small video about the subject
5. The second station: several documents about the
   topic with guiding questions

6. The third station: music/art/culture related to the topic

7. The fourth station: a web-based virtual tour of a museum or a virtual field trip to the site with observation questions.

8. Last 10 minutes of class: devote time to having the students record their work in collaboration in teams by mixing up the station groups (jigsaw method).

9. Ask the students to develop a website, or podcast, or other form of product.

So that was the worst lesson ever. I want to make sure no one ever does it again.

How do you come back from a flopped lesson?
Tweet about it using **#ThinkingAboutTeachingBook**

6. RISING ABOVE

*T*he thin envelopes of college admissions, the skinny emails of journal rejections...we all experience the pain and the trauma of missing out on a goal that we had hoped for.

Yet we move on, we rebound, and we try. We hear about grit, resilience, and can-do attitudes. One of the most critical parts of failure is the learning that emerges.

I must confess, I did not land a research award I had applied for. It was a bit painful. The feedback in the letter was helpful, and I hoped the next year to try again. I needed the feedback to expose the flaws in my thinking.

But even more, I needed the support of my loved ones. My network is strong, it is present, and it is incredible! I think about this, and I realize, after 15+ years in education, that many K-12 and higher ed students do not have this luxury.

For educators, it becomes our duty to become part of our students' networks. Before you hand back a paper, be considerate of your learner. Remember, the students do not have your experiences. If a paper or a test is really not meeting standards, do not treat it as a final submission. Instead, first, have students give peer review feedback.

A powerful learning experience is learning from your mistakes. Help students see that through Cognitive Coaching and modeling (Batt, 2010). That is the power of the teaching experience: not the grade, but the process.

What is Cognitive Coaching? It is a thinking process that the teacher models for the students. It demonstrates how we go about defining a problem, identifying ways that it can be tackled, lining up resources, and following through on the problem. I have found that we are good as a profession in teaching content, but not so good at problem-solving. Our students wonder in amazement how adults can solve a problem. All that needs to happen is the continuous demonstration of how professionals think like a problem solver.

I recommend two readings for my friends. The first is from the Chronicle of Higher education (Savani, 2016). It describes a college professor who realized that students were struggling with some issues above and beyond content. The students were struggling with life (Savani, 2016). Taking time to talk to the students about life is critical. To seek time to make that connection and then help students as they tackle course content is relevant and necessary today.

The second is a book for K-12 educators about grading practices. ASCD has some great resources. Fisher and Frey (2014) ask professionals to take time and talk with their students. Further, the authors provide recommendations on how to make sure your class is keeping up with you during the day's lessons. As instructors, we teach humans, not content. There is no download. Learning is the process of fighting battles.

There has been an explosion in discussions around "grit" recently. In academic circles, the discussions concerning grit, and students' abilities to master grit have come to dominate many discussions. Angela Duckworth's (2016) book *Grit* defines the ability of a person to overcome obstacles and not become derailed in the process as "grit." The ability to recover from a setback and move on is seen as a great asset to people. After all, how terrible is it that one setback can have ramifications for a person's entire life (Duckworth, 2016)?

Carolyn Dweck has also weighed into the discussion, with work on the concept of a "Growth Mindset" or the ability to see failure as a learning opportunity. In this work, sweeping the education nation, successful people use failure as a learning experience. Every failure is an opportunity to grow into a more proficient individual. People who follow the "growth mindset" are more adjusted to recover after a failure and see themselves as individuals who have strengths that are always under development. These people contrast with "fixed mindsets." A person who subscribes to failure as a personal statement of their negative worth finds the world difficult. They do not see self-improvement as a journey; instead it is a predetermined set level. You have it, or you don't. For many students, struggling with seeing failure as a growth opportunity happens early. The school testing system, which makes all answers right or wrong, prevents children from seeing themselves as evolving individuals. Instead, the children are treated to alpha and numeric ratings on "meeting the standards" or "does not meet the standards." This is in direct opposition to "progressing to the standard" and "progressing to a more difficult standard." The last pair is a better example of a growth mindset than what currently exists (Dweck, 2008).

As professional educators, we need to be very careful about grit, growth mindset, and grading students. We need to, as a profession, figure out how to make sure each student finds their success, even if that means a different time frame than what our school system or testing system demands. Some professionals, like a doctor, lawyer, or physical therapist, are granted a wide range of freedom to measure how successfully a client is making progress. Teachers need this ability as well. The first way we start is by asking students in our classroom to help each other find success in low-stakes ways. Emphasize teamwork. Emphasize the interdependency. Move to a culture in the classroom that celebrates the journey!

How do you rise above the mandates imposed on us in our profession?

Tweet about it using **#ThinkingAboutTeachingBook**

7. JUNE 1

emorial Day weekend marks the beginning of the end of the school year for most New York K-12 educators. In elementary schools, the longer warm days lead to students yearning for freedom of summer. The teachers and support staff yearn for the end of the school year so that they can take a deep breath and prepare for the next year, and the next round of changes.

In the middle schools, the students have grown from post-fifth graders to sixth graders. At the opposite end, the eighth graders are now preparing for high school, and the pressures of end of course exams. In New York State, we have a standards-based end of year assessment called the Regents Exams. These are high stakes exams that determine if a child can graduate, if the school is performing well, and if the teacher is doing their job in the classroom. Classroom teachers have seen students learn the core required subjects of the New York State school curriculum. More importantly, they have helped students navigate the first of many adolescent experiences.

In high school, the teachers and students are also preparing for the Regents exams. These high-stakes exams hold two parties accountable: the students and the schools. For the students, the exams determine whether or not they receive credit towards graduation; a passing grade equals freedom, while a failing grade dooms students to summer school or repeating the course.

For the school, the results on the Regents exams will determine if it is placed into one of four levels of accountability: Good Standing, Local Assistance Plan, Low Achieving, or Reward School. Schools in Good Standing are fine. There is no issue in those schools. A Reward School is going above and beyond. It is a super achiever. The Local Assistance Plan schools are having some difficulty, while Low Achieving is the bottom of the barrel. They are the lowest-performing in the state.

Over my 15+ year career in education, I have worked with students and schools who faced difficulties with the Regents exams. During my very first year of teaching, I remember working with a student who needed to pass the Global Studies exam (also known as the Global RCT) and would work with many students who were also facing delayed graduation because they struggled on the high stakes exam. The next teaching gig, I worked with several students who needed to pass the Global RCT. When it was renamed the Global History and Geography exam in late 2000, more and more students (especially those with special needs) faced increased pressure to pass the exam.

While at the State Department of Education, I was directly responsible for working with schools on the *No Child Left Behind* accountability list. The teachers and administrators were trying so hard to end the accountability whammy.

We did data analysis. We worked on professional development. We tried Read 180. Read 180 is a computer-based remediation program that was widely adopted to help students read and comprehend better. But then we realized we missed the most essential part of the process: the students.

The students never knew how they did on an exam, except for a numerical score. The students heard they failed, but never knew why they failed. They never understood what part of the exam they needed to do better on to pass.

When I had the chance to lead a wonderful group of teachers in one of the most extensive urban settings in New York, we started to change business as usual. We told the students what they were missing. We worked on their writing skills. One of our schools, working with some of the most at-risk students in the district, emphasized on-demand data feedback. Most importantly, we helped the students see patterns and have better faith in themselves. How did we accomplish this task? By going for thinking. We asked students to work out problems by wondering aloud. We asked the classes to think way beyond the test and seek ways to be creative. Our work engaged students by giving real-world problems, not just worksheets. As the students became more confident, we had them help each other. Some became experts in one sliver of content. They then would tutor classmates in reading and writing around that content area.

At the time of this writing, we are a month away from the exam. For the next 30 days, as our students are worried and nervous, we need to, as the adults, reaffirm the Growth Mindset (Dweck, 2008) idea that knowledge is learned. Learning is a process, and believing that you learn from every experience, even ones that would be considered "failures" by others, helps you become better as a learner. Second, students should be learning from small bets (Sims, 2013). This is the idea that small steps allow people to learn so much more and to retain that information. But more importantly, we need to remind students that the exams are only a tiny part of who they are.

To all of the hardworking educators out there, best of luck. To the students, do your best. To parents, support your educators and children. They need it.

How do you manage the demands of testing, without compromising your teaching?
Tweet your reflections to **#ThinkingAboutTeachingBook**

8. THE END OF THE SEMESTER

While writing this piece, I reflect upon the end of the semester. As an instructor, I suppose my teaching has translated into some learning by students in my classes and their interactions with each other. I have to confess; I learned a lot from my students as well.

First, I have learned that try as we may, students are driven to learn about life more than our content. They seek to understand the world around their lives, in which they lead and help each other lead.

Second, I have learned that taking five minutes to wave, say hello, and catch up is so critical. People need to be recognized as more than a face in the crowd, but as individuals. Wong and Wong's *First Days of School* (2009) discusses the needs people possess. Remember your Maslow? After the initial safety, food, shelter at the bottom of the pyramid, belonging is next. People, especially students, want to feel if their presence matters in society and the world. Our ever-increasing online world limits the connection and engagement that older generations took for granted when experiences emerged from day-to-day life. Our students need community, and they need someone to be supportive and present in their daily lives. Simon Sinek (2014) talks about leading people with their hearts as much more effective leadership techniques than leading a person with reason. Your students, your people, need you to recognize their existence and be present in the moment. One kind word, one wave, a smile, or a nod can brighten someone's day immensely.

Third, sometimes, you need to stop and reflect. Many instructors are great at final assessments, less so about formative assessments (Dolin, Black, Harlen, & Tiberghien, 2018). What does this mean? Final, or summative, assessments are high-stakes exams or projects which are designed to measure what you have learned throughout a period. The exams or assessments are measured against an absolute standard. There is little or no learning emerging from these assessments for the learner. These assessments mark the end, the finale. Did you get it or not? If so, how well did you get it?

A formative assessment is a growth tool. Based upon what a learner needs to know at the end of the course, how is the process going? For a student, a formative assessment can point out an area of concern that is holding back progress. These checkpoints can help both practitioners and learners be better at their roles if feedback in cold hard data can be accepted, and growth is the goal. An example: why do runners keep split times when racing? To measure their progress towards the end goal. Each section of a race is one part of the total, but a runner may need to speed up or slow down based upon their own personal goals. Remember, feedback is a gift if you choose to use it that way (Power, 2014).

If we as a profession in K-12 and higher education spent more time guiding, and less time grading, our mandate to prepare students for 21st-century skills, college and career readiness, and civics would be almost certainly met.

To the seniors I have worked with this past semester, may you achieve dreams and improve reality.

To the sophomores I have worked with, I wish you moments of joy and laughter as you pursue your education.

To the juniors, may this transition be smooth and supported.

Our dear first-year students, keep in mind that college is so different than high school. Your successes and failures are not "it," but rather the start of something amazing!

To my friends in education, keep doing well for others.

If you are a technical student, military or employed, thank you for your efforts, and keep working hard!

What is your routine to close out the end of a school year?
#ThinkingAboutTeachingBook

9. SUMMER SOCIETY

*A*s a youngster growing up in a lovely suburb, I looked forward to summer. It meant freedom from school—freedom to be outside or to read. I loved reading. One of my favorite series is the Astrowitches (Place, 1984) series that no one, I repeat *no one,* has heard of.

What's more, I loved the ability to laze around the house or the pool or the outside with friends. It was the best to run around our two acres in Orchard Park/Hamburg or the 10 acres that we lived on in Gloversville. When I was even younger, I remember going to my friend's apartment just down the block, where we could ride bikes around the cul-de-sacs for the development. It was heaven!

Later in life, I went to summer camp as a scout, first in 1988 to Scouthaven, the scout summer camp in the Buffalo, NY area. My first year at camp was cool—on the trail to first class, I learned how to cut wood properly, tie knots, and master the Blue (or highest) swimmer level requirements.

Back in my day, we earned skill awards. You needed Citizenship and one other skill award to complete Tenderfoot, the first rank in scouting. At camp, I earned swimming and one other skill award, first aid. I also was proud that I received the Fishing Merit badge. That summer was so much fun, singing songs, going to activities, and hanging out with the guys in Troop 4 from Armor, NY (a hamlet at the crossroads of Orchard Park and Hamburg).

In 1989, I again went to camp, this time to Schoellkopf Scout Reservation (SSR), out near Alden, NY, as Camp Scouthaven had been closed due to some issue. SSR was a different type of camp. When it was open, many troops went there to cook in the site. Scouthaven had a dining hall for meals. At the new camp, a large white dining tent, like a circus tent, shaded us from the rain and heat of the day to eat our three meals.

Our troop was situated in Creekside site, along the mighty Cayuga Creek. There I earned another set of merit badges. This time the Ecology section was my home. That summer, I tackled Environmental Science, Swimming, Basketry, and the Mammal Study merit badge. These four badges represented my start towards Eagle Scout.

Earlier that spring, I had earned the First Aid merit badge, and in the process, completed all of the eight skill award requirements for first class. This is the midway point on a

Scouts Trail to Eagle. It marks a step when a young person becomes a leader in the troop. At home, my second class rank requirements were met by the Music merit badge and American Heritage merit badge. My hobbies and interests were beginning to shine—I liked history and environmental sciences.

Over the years, I was exposed to several different merit badges and learned quite a bit about a lot. Looking at what students in rural or urban poverty face, most students are by no means exposed to the camps and hobbies, interests, or fascinating experiences of merit badges. In one location, where I worked for a year and a half (two summer sessions), students who attended summer school were subjected to crunch summer school sessions of the same content as to what they experienced during the year.

The classes were held in a hot (80+ degree building) with poor tasting water, little air movement, and stifling humidity. Everyone in the classroom was in survival mode due to the heat. Movies were shown or video clips, so the lights were kept off. Teachers and students were in unbearable conditions because some places won't pay for air conditioning in schools. It's a luxury after all—even if we see record-breaking summers due to climate change (Fleming et al., 2018). The lunches were sub-par—two slices of bread, a slice of processed cheese, and a slice of processed meat. One kid remarked, "we got better food in juvie."

Yeah, it's true.

What we feed our poor kids in many poor schools is crappy carb- and sugar-rich foods. Breakfast for the summer usually entailed a juice, cereal, and chocolate or strawberry milk. Yep—sugar comas in 20 minutes.

Over and over, I oversaw state efforts and federal programs, and in the cities, the activities were all school-related. One of the most significant changes we as an educational profession need to make is the idea that a camp is a requirement, not a luxury, for children. What might happen in a poor environment? At the end of June when school lets out, many of our students living in poverty are faced with summer school. Or a teen may be responsible for caring for a brother or sister, or multiple family members. Not all high poverty areas may have these problems. We must, however, as a society, find a way to level the playing field between my experience and that of a poor inner-city or rural student.

How can you help to level the playing field for all students, regardless of zip code?

Tweet about it using **#ThinkingAboutTeachingBook**

10. BACK TO SCHOOL

The end of summer heralds back to school. It is the end of summer school, the end of camps, and the beginning of sales for school essentials. K-12 teachers are working on finishing their professional development assignments. Lesson and unit plans are reshaped in anticipation of the new year. College students are ready for dorm life. College faculty are readying syllabi and assignments.

For some students, back to school means back to regular meals and freedom from the streets of their neighborhoods. A book to consider, *Ain't No Makin It (*MacLeod, 2018*)*, considered the communities some of our students live in. The poverty of urban and rural America has created a situation where the summer brain drain causes our students to lose two months of learning and miss another one month as teachers try to ramp the learning back up (Alexander, Entwisle, & Olson, 2007). In households higher on the socioeconomic ladder, like ones Sean Reardon (2011) has studied, children have a wide variety of camps and activities that they can undertake to stall the summer learning gap and actually add to their experience bank.

If we, as a society, would like our students to be successful, we must provide free, safe, and unstructured play in the summer for students. Children love to play. The freedom of play allows kids to explore their world, to make up adventures, and to see different endings to stories. Imagination in play is really critical!

We must value the work our educators do by not stating that summer is their "vacation time." It is, for many, their only time for professional development and recovery.

We must also give students rich learning experiences. How can we do these things?

First, our local museums and historical sites must have the level of funding they need to run summer programs. There are so many beautiful museums and historical places that do not have the funding to open when families can visit or stay open seven days a week. I wish that the different levels of government and private donors give much-needed funds to cover basic operating expenses to allow museums to remain open seven days a week for at least 12 hours a day. For example, our state museum is open for six days a week, from 9:30 am-

5:00 pm. Further, money should be restored to schools and museums to allow field trips to help engage student learning. Marcus, Stoddard, and Woodward (2017), in their book about museums and schools, indicated there is a strong connection between learning retention and museum experience. We must pay heed. Utilize the museums and the programs that are running to explore life. Move museum experiences and displays into your pedagogy.

Second, we must make the community-based organization camps like the YMCA and the BSA and GSUSA more widely utilized. Our community groups have great programs about history, science, and civic engagement. Scouts and YMCA provide some of the most powerful and influential experiences that children can take part in, but so many programs are under-subscribed. Did you know that the Boy Scouts of America has summer camp opportunities for children ages 6-21? The average cost of a week at camp is $400. This includes a place to stay Sunday to Saturday, three square meals a day, and over 40 + activities for a young person to enjoy. The YMCA week at camp costs $350 a week. The Girl Scouts are in a similar range. There are great experiences, and there are hundreds more throughout the community.

If the government were genuinely interested in increased educational achievement, they would fund summer activities which are not summer schools, but summer adventures. Peter Dewitt in Edweek (2016) discussed the differences between

Finland and the US in terms of educational outputs. One point stood out: in Finland, education, of all types, is valued. In the US, we should increase summer programming for all children that is adventure-expeditionary based.

How do you recharge over summer break?
Tweet about it using **#ThinkingAboutTeachingBook**

11. FAVORITE BOOKS

*I*n education, we often are asked how to get children to read. Books start at picture book levels, and then move up to chapter books, and finally end at novels. Today (at the time of writing) marks the 20th anniversary of Harry Potter, and this has caused me to think about which books I liked to read as I grew up. Reading became a constant companion of mine and allowed me to explore the world beyond my own life. Books are my addiction. Erasmus is my hero:

"When I have a little money, I buy books; and if I have any left, I buy food and clothes."

Mom and Dad indulged my reading habit with abandon. Scholastic book fairs and Book-It would cost a lot of money, and now in reflection, it was really too much. B Dalton,

Barnes and Noble, and even used bookstores should have sold us stock. We would have been rich! Our house had books aplenty, and a good number of magazines and newspapers. We had P*opular Science, Discovery Magazine*, and a whole host of others, including *National Geographic*. Words were everywhere in our house. I don't remember which picture books I liked, but one of my first favorite characters was Dumbo from the Disney franchise (1941). There was just something about that elephant that made me so happy.

As a young boy, I loved to read, so I devoured books. *Encyclopedia Brown* was one series that was so exceptional. The crime-fighting, the use of logic, reasoning, and the knowledge the E.B. displayed in the books. His skilled sidekicks, who should have had their own starring role! The son of a local police chief, the kid who solved crimes through the use of an encyclopedic brain and memory. They used forensic techniques, deductive logic, and an evident reliance on the town's resources. Such a fun and fantastic adventure for a young boy to read. This series led me to love reading and instilled in me a desire to solve puzzles.

Who doesn't love a little fiction with a vampire bunny? *Bunnicula* (Howe & Howe, 1979) and the series about the vampire bunny sparked a love in me of the supernatural and the dynamics of family and pets. My family had a rabbit, a dog, and a cat, all at the same time. You have to love the mystery of it all, trying to figure out who drained the celery of its essential elements? The simple, quiet bunny? These adventures with anthropomorphic animals were undoubtedly more interesting than some of the reading materials the school provided. Such mystery surrounded the innocent bunny and the other mischievous characters within the series.

Every once in a while (ok, a lot), I read books that surprised or confused my teachers at school. When I was in fourth or fifth grade, the teacher in our English block asked what our favorite book was. I replied, T*he First Astrowitches* (Place, 1984). The teacher did a double-take. "Could you repeat that?"

I loved a book about two witch children who made their way into outer space on the space shuttle. Her series on the witches were all about a young person growing into their own, solving big problems and little problems. Such an enjoyable series.

The Mouse and Motorcycle (Cleary, 1965) stands out in my mind as a book I loved to read. Ralph Mouse, the star of the books, helped and looked over his family and his home. The books had fun and adventure, and they explored the idea of helping people. Cleary's works, including *Ramona the Pest* (Cleary, 1968), became one of those series you just had to follow. Between the two series, I became a devoted fan of her writings, and I continue to believe that her works set many members of my generation down the right path.

I would be remiss if I did not mention Judy Blume and her

Tales of a Fourth-Grade Nothing (1972), *Superfudge* (1980), and *Freckle Juice* (1971). Her books looked at moving, a new baby in the family, and all of those events which fourth-graders go through, especially if they are the oldest in the family. These classic series allow the reader to empathize, take a different perspective, and in other works, deal with critical issues.

One of the most crucial series I read was *Star Trek* novels. This is where life got expensive. They were add-ons to the TOS and TNG TV programs. My best friend in elementary school, Rick Schaus, introduced me to the love of Trek. They were adventurous, formulaic, and just awesome! Reading these books let me escape and enjoy reading.

Jody Lynn Nye's *Mythology* books (1990) were great reads —the scholarly nature of studying magic, the adventures, and the drama were all such amazing parts of the series about Mythology and its happenings. I really enjoyed it when the protagonist was launched into a situation where they had to solve problems or use their wits and knowledge to fight the bad guys (Nye,1990).

C. Dale Brittan's *A Bad Spell in Yurt* (1991) is another series of outstanding novels. Graduating from Wizard College, a young man moves to a small kingdom to solve crises and become a hero. Nicely written and fantastic in its characterization as well as story arch, I loved the Yurt novels for their adventure, use of magic, and more importantly, the scholarly nature of the protagonist.

Finally, my heart still weeps at the loss of Tom Clancy. The cold-war *Hunt for Red October* (1985) and all of the rest of the works he wrote were just amazing. They combined drama, politics, and when I harbored a fascination with the navy, a glimpse into the life. Such a dynamic and fantastic series of books. So much drama with geopolitical and personal conflict. With its omnipresent narrator, you wanted to know why people weren't supporting the bigger picture and needs.

These books were creative and held passion and drama. I read a study (Perrin, 2018) that many adults just stop reading after school. I also found that many kids find reading to be a chore. It's true...the damn accountability system has beaten the love of reading out of many children. When you are forced to take an Accelerated Reader test to prove you read a book, then what the hell—too much accountability for what is, in essence, a leisure activity. Tom Clancy never intended THRO to be testable! So why did we as an educational system make THRO, and other books, subject to multiple-choice? Let's recapture the magic by allowing greater choice in reading. Let's help parents, children, families, and adults to regain the love of and for reading. As teachers, I challenge you to create a list of favorite books to share with your class.

A book I love: _____

Why do I love it? _____

Tweet about your experience using
#ThinkingAboutTeachingBook

12. ONE FOR DATA

*D*ata, data, data. The plural of datum, or a character on *Star Trek, The Next Generation* (Nemecek, 2003)? The bane of grad students' existence everywhere? A way for the state to impose its ideals on schools. No! Data is part of a toolset every educator should know and be able to use.

Do we, as educators, really look at data that our students generate for us? Let's take absenteeism. If members of your class are late or absent on a particular day all the time, is it a coincidence or a pattern? Could it be that the student is always absent on Monday due to transition patterns in a split family (one parent on the weekend, one during the week)? Are secondary students late because they work a job at night and are very tired?

How about teacher-generated data-collecting instruments (quizzes and tests)? Do we examine results question-by-question? Is time taken to look at a gap analysis and figure out which of the wrong answers really were wrong answers, or faulty logic when students thought about a problem?

I previously presented at the NYSCSS Conference about the use of data analysis in the classroom. One key finding in my research was the student interview portion (qualitative) part is almost always forgotten by teachers in the analytic process. Here are my suggestions.

1. Talk to the students (at least three—one is an event, two could be a coincidence, three is a pattern).
2. Have them walk through their thinking on a question they chose the wrong answer to.

This will serve two purposes: a) helping the student understand the right answer, and b) helping you craft a lesson that will head off the incorrect thinking before the summative assessment (test).

Classroom strategies concerning peer tutoring stress having peer tutors work with each other to "reclaim" instructional time that can fritter away when the teacher focuses on whole-class instruction. I recommend that teachers explore research concerning classwide peer tutoring strategies and utilize it in the classroom to help students work together in teams. There are two significant benefits to this approach:

1. Students are growing into a world which expects teamwork and team engagement from day one in the workplace. Forbes, Inc, Business, and other trade journals have all written about how to build and motivate teams.

2. Students will see learning from peers as an excellent resource. In higher education and the workforce, informal learning teams, not focused on the professor or supervisor, are the norm in many places. A team approach to problem-solving with peers is expected behavior in many work environments.

Classwide Peer Tutoring Set Up

1. Have students identify concepts with which they are unfamiliar. Limit this to ten for the first round.

2. Identify teams of no more than six students to work in pairs against at least one other team of the same size.

3. Have the students write a concept on a 3 x 5" index card. Then have the students free draw an image that represents the concept on the front of the card. Repeat this step for each of the 10 concepts.

4. On the back of the card, have the students define

the concept. Have the students give one example
on the bottom of the back of the card.

5. Punch one hole in the corner of each card and have
   the students reinforce the hole. Then have the
   students place a zip tie from the grocery store or a
   metal ring to tie the group of cards together.

6. Have the teams of six break up into pairs. The
   students then go through each of the cards. They
   earn a point for each card they get right. As a class,
   record all of the points in a competition. On Friday,
   hold a round-robin tournament. The winner of the
   point totals for the week gets a coupon to use for a
   free homework or a re-do on an assignment.

7. After the students have mastered the cards,
   students develop a new stack. After five weeks,
   bring the old stack out. Each unit should result in
   new team formations.

THIS PROCESS HAS WORKED VERY SUCCESSFULLY. I
personally have used it in my classroom. This is a fun and
engaging activity for students to take in class, out of class, or
in study halls.

How do you use peer tutoring in your classroom?
Tweet about it using **#ThinkingAboutTeachingBook**

13. ATTEMPTING GRANTS

*A*s a young academic, I hear a lot of advice and read a lot of websites on how to win grants. It seems money to support education research is being directed into areas that are the priority of the funding agents, not the scholars. Hess' book on *Philanthropy in Education* (2005) is so very critical and essential to read. Especially with No Child Left Behind (NCLB) and Every Student Succeeds Act (ESSA), it seems that education is no longer a route to equality, but rather a way to divide people even further by economics. Children in different schools receive an education based upon, in my observations, the zip code. My experience in rural education saw our work as a team of teachers struggling against the realities of poverty and disengagement every day. Reflecting on my own lived school experience, I had the benefit of technology, parent scaffolding, and course work, which was on par with college expectations. In some of the rural schools in which I worked, this was not true—our students did not have classes that would prepare their future paths.

At the time of this writing, I am embarking on an attempt to win a grant, which will serve to help facilitate teachers in social studies working as a group to discuss literacy in the classroom. The grant was moderately successful! My research and work with teachers will hopefully reach at-risk students, and most in need of the scholarly abilities that will help them learn historical literacy. In the fall, we will hopefully have a Professional Learning Community that will involve the reading of Nokes's work on Historical Literacy (2013). I was able to offer a scaled-down version of the grant and presented a day-long workshop on how to use literacy in social studies classrooms! It was inspiring to see the five teachers (virtually) chat and message back and forth on the topic of literacy.

Grant writing can be frustrating, and the expertise required to write a successful grant may not be learned easily. I would encourage you, as a reader and student of the art of teaching, to go to a local bookstore and look for a text on writing grants. It will help your classroom, and you as a teacher!

Have you ever written grants for your classroom, school, or district?

Tweet your best tips using **#ThinkingAboutTeachingBook**

14. INVESTING IN EDUCATION

*T*here is an old saying that a house is the most substantial investment in a person's life. I would like to change this thought to be the investment in public education. See, the property and income taxes a person pays, especially in New York, are a more significant investment than the purchase of a house. We invest in our communities. We support our schools. More importantly, we need to ensure as a community that we support our students.

At the time of this writing, our students in New York State are taking Regents Exams. They have invested their time, talent, and sweat into the year. On the flip side, our teachers gave even more. They gave their time, talent, effort, and in many instances, their treasure to ensure our students were ready. This included spending their own money to make sure school supplies arrived in the hands of every student and bringing in their own books to classrooms. I, for one, used to buy vacation souvenirs to use in my classroom. My family and friends gifted me with classroom artifacts for social studies as well!

We also can't forget the administration, the support staff, and the volunteers. The administrators are up late, often into the evening or early checking emails, writing a parent, or opening the door for a student dropped off way too early. Also, we must celebrate the support staff, cleaners, bus drivers, TAs, and aides who do the work that isn't tested but is critical to the students, the teachers, and the BOE. Finally, we salute the volunteers, who come into the School Board of Education members, or tutors, or people who make sure the musical is ready to go.

But we also need to remember our community librarians, museums, and other professionals and service folks who help out our students on their educational paths. As communities, we need to do a better job supporting each other. One of my colleagues wrote a fantastic PhD dissertation on K-16 cradle to career networks (Zuckerman, 2016). It is a must-read dissertation on efforts to work between community and schools.

In rural areas especially, the connection between school and communities are so close. A great piece by Maria Tieken (2014) dives very deeply into the rural school and community relationship. In the 2018-2019 period, many works on rural areas appeared in press and in online formats. Too numerous to mention, your school or neighborhood librarian can help you find some great resources on the topic, and help you learn the successful recipes for excellence!

We need to invest in education because, in many instances, it is the only investment in many rural communities. To ensure strength in these communities, states need to prioritize rural education and fund it in such a way that all students can succeed, whether that means going to college, getting a job, learning a trade, or buying a house in a community to invest in education.

In many areas, taxes are a huge issue, but so is the school budget. As students move into adulthood, they need to be informed about how education finance works. For my state, in particular, New York, the easy answer is it's complicated! So, questions must emerge within the classroom about how to support education, how the school budget works, and why decisions are made based upon available information. Students need information about the process. I would like to encourage you, as a teacher to work with your fellow teachers in career education and begin the process by asking a real estate agent to visit the school and discuss with your students how real estate works. This beginning of a unit will allow students a grasp or handle on some of the decisions which many will face as adults in or beyond the local community.

One business teacher I know has told me that in their class, students do not understand really how the economy works. This is a critical area of support that students need to know about. It stems from relevance and how students and their parents view education. With the rise of unstructured economies, gig jobs, and a whole host of disruptions, I know I feel unprepared to face tomorrow! Several students will need help with the economy. There is hope—as we use our collective knowledge and skill, and experience to help students see how best to thrive. Maybe our children will move to small business or craft-based industries. Maybe corporate culture will give way to community-based economics. Who knows, let us be optimistic!

STEP ONE:

Ask students to experience a simulation with you (Vandsburger, Duncan-Daston, Akerson, & Dillon, 2010). Contact your United Way to get *The Game of Life* information. The United Way's program will help students understand an economic reality which they will face soon. In my humble opinion, *The Game of Life* is much better suited than the stock market game, which many economics classes play.

STEP TWO:

Have students switch up existence once every week and report on how moving up or down on the ladder impacted their decision making.

. . .

STEP THREE:

Have students identify a service project to help the community address one of the issues which emerged while playing *The Game of Life*.

How can you engage your students in authentic problem-based learning?

Tweet your ideas to **#ThinkingAboutTeachingBook**

15. SCHOOL BUDGET VOTE

*T*he expression that "all politics is local" (Tip O'Neill, former Speaker of the US House) rings so true, now that, at the time of this writing, the school budget vote is upon us in New York State. The yearly exercise of the franchise is one of the most exceptional features in American Federal Democracy. In America, the 10th Amendment of the Bill of Rights returns to the states any powers not reserved to the federal government or denied to the states. Education falls under this provision.

In New York State, the final say of power within the local school district is the voters. Today, school budgets were put up to vote. Candidates for the local school board sought election to a mostly-volunteer position of public service. The civic duty of voting during a school budget election (or for Board of

Education representatives) is critical to how a school district enacts education within its boundaries.

I wanted to take this moment and thank school board members, both past and present, for the services that they have rendered in local communities across the state. From the smallest district of Raquette Lake to the largest districts of the "Big 5," the five city school districts (New York, Yonkers, Syracuse, Rochester, and Buffalo), many hours are spent trying to make sure budgets are crafted correctly, the best teachers are hired, and the greatest number of children have the best education possible. While there is a way to go in many places, the passion of BOE members is palpable.

If you are interested, there is a wide variety of resources available on the jobs of a BOE member. The New York State School Boards Association (NYSSBA) has a website devoted to the calling of School Board members. Dr. John Sipple has developed a wealth of resources for citizens and school board members at the New York State Center for Rural Schools. If you are interested in learning more, please go to their sites.

The critical nature of voting and information literacy has, in recent years, become the topic *du jour* for many educators. We strive, as a profession, to educate, and a vital part of this role is to help our students make sense of information and where, especially at the local level, the source emerged. As a middle or high school lesson connection for supporting schools and information literacy in general, I offer the following suggestion:

Lesson Connections

Start by asking students to rate on a scale of trustworthy to questionable places where they get information. I offer the following ideas:

- The social media platform of the day, such as Twitter, Facebook, or Snapchat
- Their friends
- The local newspaper
- The local TV or radio station
- A regional newspaper
- National news sites
- Podcasts
- Wikipedia

Have students research how these sources of news gather their information. How does the editor select news for placement? How do the "on-air personalities" or presenters make their choices on what stories are read or run?

Give students a famous event from history from multiple perspectives. Ask the students to identify the competing views and competing narratives. I would recommend the decision to enter World War I, as the centennial remembrance has just passed.

Ask the students what types of sources the author used to tell the events. Where they actually present? If so, what was the author's alignment politically or economically or socially?

Did the author of the report have a corroborating source, or are they the "lone voice?" Was the author trying to persuade others to their side of the story?

Ask the students to then take a side—which set of documents do they believe and why? Have the students provide examples. Ask the students to discuss the author's purpose and why they think the purpose was communicated effectively or ineffectively. Cite examples.

Have the students present their judgment and rationale on historic media literacy and then ask the students to build a lesson for elementary students. If your school has one, connect with the librarian to help facilitate this work.

How do you promote information literacy with your students? Tweet your best tips using **#ThinkingAboutTeachingBook**

16. STUDENT TEACHING AND UNPAID INTERNSHIPS

*a*s the school year ended and a legion of student teachers left the classroom, a question emerged in my mind as I drove from Rochester to Albany. Listening to NPR, there was a lively debate on the role of using unpaid internships in business as unethical and exploitative. Should schools and schools of education be concerned as well (Ahmed, 2011)?

Student teaching asks college students in their final year to assume classroom status as a "practicing teacher," working in a public school to educate children under the NCLB/RTTT/CCLS/ESSA (all of these letters are reform acronyms) world, one which holds teachers accountable for the tests their students will take this year.

As a student-teacher back in the 1990s, I saw how this effort was extremely tiring as I used my intellectual energy just so I could receive 15 credits (which I paid for) on a pass/fail basis. My cooperating teachers turned over all aspects of the classroom to me, including the prep work and the grading, as well as the teaching, for usually a total of 8 weeks.

This unpaid internship was designed to allow me to experience the rigors of teaching in a classroom. I learned a lot.

Thank goodness my parents allowed me to live at home (rent-free), fed me, and gave me money for gas, insurance, and repairs for my car, all so I could travel five days a week for 15 weeks to an unpaid internship. If I had been receiving financial aid, would that have covered the rent, groceries, and gas money, I was expected to pay to undertake this internship? It would have, but I would need to pay back financial aid and the interest associated with the borrowing.

Division I sports are considering paying/ increasing aid for their athletes. Should student teachers receive the same benefits?

In this day and age of difficulty in recruiting the best and the brightest into teaching, should we reconsider the cost to the student teacher, especially when many schools of education forbid student teachers from holding outside jobs? These young professionals are forgoing income during this time, unlike their peers not in an education major, and are performing work just for in my case, a pass-fail grade and a letter of recommendation. For students with financial needs, is the unpaid internship (which may require transportation from the college to another location, the acquisition of a car, and paying for expenses not covered under grants in aid or student loans) preventing some of the best and brightest from entering the profession?

Teaching is, after all, one of the gateways to the middle class (Lampert, Burnett, & Lebhers, 2016). Research reports have shown that for many working-class families seeking to advance to the middle class, teaching and nursing are viewed as two central professions for this growth (Bui, 2014). Research into minority identifying teachers also indicates that many feel a desire to return and role model for younger members of the community what it takes to move from poverty to middle-class status (Higginbotham & Weber, 1992). Maybe the profession needs to re-think the unpaid internship status and make internships paid like many other professions And yet the SUNY and NYSED leadership have indicated we have a teacher shortage. If teachers cannot have loans forgiven, then how can we serve the public?

One way the educational and governmental system could help teachers is via free tuition, room, expenses, and associated education costs similar to athletic scholarships. Athletes at many Division I institutions receive some form of aid for performing on the field (Lough, 2016). Teachers could benefit from receiving tuition waivers and residency expense waivers. Another example of front-end cost reduction is the total subsidization of education schools by the government for national defense purposes. As some educational historians have shown, following the launch of Sputnik by the former Soviet Union, the US Government increased aid to colleges to ramp up science, tech, world language, and math teacher training (Reese, 2011). If education is really as critical as some politicians lead Americans to believe, why doesn't our investment match the rhetoric?

BREAK AND REFLECT:

1. As a novice, mid-career, or experienced teacher, what are some areas of your entry into the profession that could have gone better?
2. How can you, personally and in your organization, do more to improve the experience new teachers have entering the profession?

Tweet your reflections to **#ThinkingAboutTeachingBook**

17. MENTORS AND MENTORING

*a*s I was working in my office at home today, I came across some mentoring books from my time at University at Buffalo, where I finished the Advanced Certificate in Teacher Mentoring program. We read and discussed a wide range of articles and books on mentoring. We explored why teachers become mentors. More importantly, we looked at what an effective mentoring program should look like. State University of New York (SUNY) and the New York State Education Department (NYSED) have announced that a teacher shortage will soon happen in New York state. We will have difficulty recruiting teachers in the field, but we need to remember one of the critical features of teacher recruitment is retention.

The induction process starts with recruitment. Luke Miller, in the *Journal of Research in Rural Education*, found that in

New York, several teachers wish to remain as close to home as possible. This primarily affects rural schools, where recruitment is difficult. Boyd, Lankford, Loeb, & Wyckoff (2005) have researched the quality of teacher candidates recruited into the field. Higher quality teachers help students achieve more and quicker than other teachers who are mediocre. Further, teachers who are poor-quality, according to their study, negatively impact children in the class at a higher rate than the high-performing teachers help children. Other researchers, including reports from *EdWeek,* and others, including The New Teacher Project (Moore Johnson, 2004), have found many teachers only stay in the profession for five years.

Five years.

One extra year than a high school student takes to graduate.

Five years.

The length of time many students take to complete a bachelor's degree.

In those five years, districts invest significant resources in providing teachers professional development. They may provide a mentor to the teachers for one year. I don't know about you, but I still need mentors, almost 20+ years after I graduated from high school and went to work in my professional field.

Education needs mentors to work with new teachers. We need the retirees who still have something to give to help ease the burden of practicing professionals in the trenches themselves. In a *Chronicle of Higher Ed* article (June, 2016), emeritus professors are hoping to give back to their institutions. Maybe it's time for K-12 education to name emeritus teachers and administrators in an effort to gather their energy, knowledge, experience, and resources for use in our resource-poor districts in the rural and urban areas. Right now, mentoring resources for many schools are stretched pretty thin. As new teachers come into the profession, and experienced teachers retire, why not hire retired teachers on sub pay to help mentor new teachers? Give the new teachers a lot more support, such as a co-teacher—someone in the room to help make sure they survive the first few years of trial and error. Why waste all that great experience when it walks out the door? My neighbor is thrilled that she retired from teaching. She doesn't want to be done-done. She wants to help newer teachers and give back to the kids, not just during the daily grind of teaching. I could see lists of teachers collected and distributed regionally. Districts need some stability by having experienced folks help out new folks. Oh, and at the administrative level, it's done all the time. Shift some funding into the teacher ranks to make a better education project!

On a personal note, one of my first mentors, Mr. Larry Wrobelewski, the Associate Editor of the *Polish American Journal*, passed away from cancer the night before I wrote this section. Larry was a great friend and mentor, and for 24 years served as one of my constant sources of inspiration. Rest in peace, Mr. W. We have the trail from here.

Question: can you identify what stresses occur in your life as a novice teacher, a mid-career teacher, or a seasoned teacher? Let's try an exercise together:

If I had known

_____ when I first

started teaching I would have

_____.

The hardest part about my early career in teaching is

_____.

The easiest part about my early career in teaching is

_____.

I admire _____ 's teaching ability and I want to know more about how they implement _____ in their classroom.

From the moment I wake up until sleep arrives, I worry about

_____.

I wake up every morning looking forward to

_____.

This summer I want to focus on

_____ as a way to

better prepare for _____.

I am going to do the following to get ready for summer:

_____.

I am going to do the following to get ready for tomorrow:

_____.

I am going to do the following during the weekend:

_____.

Next month I will

_____.

I have become so skilled at

_____, that I want

to share this with others. Therefore, I will do

_____ as a way to share

my knowledge.

One classroom practice I can change is

_____ to free up

time for me to concentrate on_____.

On a scale of 1 to 10, with 1 being not proud, and 10 being

proud, how happy am I with my teaching?_____

On a scale of 1 to 10, how satisfied am I with my home/work balance? _____

My dream vacation is:

_____.

I will bring home _____ for my classroom.

Look at these pages again in a year. See if any answers change! Tweet any *aha*s to **#ThinkingAboutTeachingBook**

18. LOSING GOOD EDUCATORS

The New York State School Boards recently published a report on how New York State can address the teaching shortage that has concerned people lately (Heiser, 2017). SUNY and New York State Education Department held a summit with the chancellors discussing ways to improve the teacher pipeline. New York State United Teachers, the teachers' union, is surveying the field on what to do to improve teacher pipelines. Both SUNY and private schools are reporting a precipitous decline in teacher education applications.

I have a better thought: why are we ignoring candidates on the market? When I was in high school, we had a substitute teacher who was always there, year after year. Granted, my school was suburban and wealthy, an easy place to teach once you entered.

One day, I asked him (as a senior would) why he kept subbing. He told me that the school administration and all the career centers at the college recommended that it was in his best interest to substitute teach.

Fast forward to today, after I have been an administrator. In some places, administrators won't hire good substitute teachers because they are so hard to find. In other places, the schools won't hire substitutes after a year or two because, as another administrator told me, that "something must be wrong with them. If they were good, they would have gotten hired already."

Let us dwell on that for a second—in teaching, we have a Goldilocks problem. We want our teacher candidates young, but experienced. We want teachers who have done stuff, but not too much stuff. We want teachers to prove their worth by subbing, but we want to have our options open. In a relationship, this would be abusive!

There is something seriously wrong with a system when some of the best, most dedicated people I know are kicked to the curb because they "don't fit the culture of a building." Are you kidding me?

What if the culture is wrong and the person is the fix?

One of my jobs at the state Department of Education was going into failing schools. They were failing because people did not do their jobs—and yet good teachers were tossed to the side because of a seniority bump, or an administrator screwed up paperwork. I have friends who have led professional development, who were told that "[they] weren't creative enough" in the classroom. Seriously? In New York State education, a law exists that defines seniority as the time you serve in a position. A candidate is appointed to one of many areas in service by the local Boards of Education, upon the recommendation of the superintendent of schools. As this teacher is working in their job, they have four years to demonstrate that as a practitioner, they are competent enough in the execution of their job to warrant tenure. Tenure is defined as the process which a district must follow to eliminate a person from their position. When a new teacher is just hired or is up for tenure, they are vulnerable to a wide range of reasons that they can be dismissed, with little recourse.

I had a friend of mine leave a tenured administrative job in a suburban district to go work in a high-need district. In the high needs district, they let him go because of budget cuts. Now he can't find work in the classroom because he has "been out of the classroom for too long."

Wait—he was an administrator in classrooms every day! How could this be?

I have another friend who was told: "your teaching philosophy doesn't fit our building." She created interactive and hands-on lessons that helped kids enjoy science. How does that deviate from a child-centered philosophy?

I have had friends move out of teaching and into administration, where the politics in the district sweep them up and dump them in a trash heap. If you are an administrator in one of the lowest-performing schools in the state, and you work every day for 12 hours to help make sure students get legally mandated required service, how can you be told you were "ineffective"? What does this mean? Can you perform a miracle?

It angers me that we claim there is a teacher shortage, and yet so many people willing to serve as teachers are told they are not wanted. How can a guy who is an internationally known trainer be told, "your teaching style was not right for our population," in math no less! We can't find math teachers! We need math teachers (Chiang, Clark, & McConnell, 2017). It was not like my friend was a Ben Stein in the classroom. This is a reference to the teacher in *Ferris Bueller's Day Off*.

In my state, the first four years of a teacher's and administrator's career are on a probationary appointment. This means they can more easily be fired. Usually, in the past, the school will ask politely for a teacher to "resign," so they have a brief opportunity to pay for all of their health care through the summer or get unemployment benefits, depending on the stance a school would take towards that teacher's claim. It's not an equal situation, and usually, the teacher's union, which will take 10% of your salary, can't do much.

If you are in an at-will employment state, you may have NO rights whatsoever. Your contract can be terminated for no reason whatsoever. This makes no sense in a profession where it takes, according to the New Teacher Project and every research article I have seen, at least five to seven years to get good (Fenstermacher & Richardson, 2005).

Let's face it, folks—our system is what is causing a shortage in teachers. We have willing people with a go-get-'em attitude, some with experience and expertise. The system, as it is currently constructed, doesn't allow for the effective distribution of labor. Quality control over who is selected and who can remain is really very situational. Some bad teachers receive tenure, and too many are let go because of some political or personality reasons. I hate to say this, but every single one of you probably knows someone great who was let go and a dud that stayed.

The evaluative system for teachers needs to look at second chances.

How can you have a second chance if the past continues to haunt you? In the HR classes and leadership readings I do for my job, I see the idea that we must work to ensure the person is the "right fit," and we "maximize human capital." I think education, in trying to be like business, has adopted the 1980s model of slash and burn (Downs, 1995), not the 2010s model of leadership and inspiration.

The education system that has taken over 100 years to develop is falling apart because too many American educators don't like to change the status quo. Our students see bullying behavior enacted every day in how the administration is treated and how it treats others. Teachers also bully each other.

The students hear this. They know it happens. Can we, as a profession, really look in the mirror and defend our behaviors?

In law, there is a saying: "I would rather let 10 guilty people go free than to jail one innocent person" (Kennedy, 1978). In education, we have apparently reversed the idea to reflect, "we would rather let 10 good teachers go so that we don't accidentally keep one bad teacher." Except we do—and kids suffer.

In the United States, we built our nation on the idea of going someplace to get a fresh start. There is no fresh start. As I look for job postings for my unemployed friends, I see this phrase: "Please provide your latest evaluation scores."

How can one come back from a negative evaluation?
#ThinkingAboutTeachingBook

19. IMPLEMENTING FRESH STARTS
   IN THE CLASSROOM

*N*ow that I've talked a little about "fresh starts" and evaluations for teachers, let's do a thought exercise for students!

Think of one student you had in the past who needed a break in your classroom.

Now, think of what they did wrong.

Now, what did YOU do as an educator to create a path of difficulty?

What could you or the student have done differently to help give them a second chance in class?

If you really are stuck, try thinking about Project-Based Learning or an alternative assignment.

OUR STUDENTS FACE INCREASINGLY OVERWHELMING PATHS every day. If we remember our dear friend Maslow's base of the triangle, the foundations include physical needs and safety. Only after those needs are fulfilled can people move to worrying about academics. We often forget that level 3 is affirmation—does someone care about the person.

I want you to remember that every child deserves an advocate. They need someone to say:

"I BELIEVE IN YOU."

"I AM GLAD YOU ARE HERE"

"YOU ARE A VALUE"

And remember—actions speak louder than words!

WHAT ACTION WILL YOU ENGAGE IN TO *SHOW* YOUR STUDENTS that they matter—even when you cannot take one more second of being in the same room?

Tweet any *aha*s to **#ThinkingAboutTeachingBook**

20. WORKING FOR THE STATE

*W*hen you are a teacher, it is quite easy to hear about "the State." After all, the regulations, the standards, the tests, and lately, the curriculum suggestions have come from "the State." The State visits schools a lot. State auditors come in to make sure policies and procedures are being followed. The State will send child nutrition experts in to look at school breakfast and lunch protocols. The State sends in monitors to look at bilingual education—does it comply with the law, with regulations? A special education visit will determine if the school is following procedures under law and regulation or a court order under a "focused review." My office visited schools as part of three primary reasons: Title I reviews, school improvement reviews, and Regents Examination protocol reviews.

The State Office of the Comptroller once sent a group of

accountants out among the schools to check on the compliance with state education regulations on the storage, administration, and correcting of Regents exams. A Regents exam comes at the end of the school year in high school. Since the 1800s, they have been used to determine how well students are prepared for college. Lately, they have been used in accountability purposes to make sure schools are doing a measurable job in graduating students from high school. They are a high stakes exam, and every child, except for a small percentage, must take and pass the tests to graduate. The state auditors found messes everywhere they went. In some districts, the exams were not appropriately secured. The state requires a locked facility to ensure that the exams are not accessible. In other places, the auditors found the proctors did not read a statement that banned electronic devices and communication instruments. One principal told me that there was no cell coverage in their town and no cell phones. The third group of problems emerged from correcting the exams. The auditors found teachers did not follow the rubric and incorrectly graded exams. So, the department sent our team, the school improvement team, out to observe and monitor the exam administration unannounced.

We wore suits because we are the State. We went into great schools, small schools, poor schools, and affluent schools. Our teams went local to Albany and across the state to Western New York, the Adirondacks, Long Island, and the City. I had the ability to visit small rural schools that were forced to convert old bathrooms into safes so they could store their exams. In the southern tier, an eight-mile drive to a local distribution point can mean blizzards and severe road conditions. I also discovered that the gyms are as hot as I remember as a kid. How can you take a high stakes exam on a muggy, 80-degree day with no wind? I was dying in my suit. The administrators were in shorts and t-shirts, the teachers were in the same. Here I was in a suit! I also found that many teachers felt the state was overburdening them with curriculum and standards changes. The teachers were frankly exhausted, turning around each year to a new mandate and a new demand from the state.

When we traveled to do a Title I review, it was a mass invasion onto the school district. SED would send at least two people from the Title I office. Then a person from Title II, professional development, Title IID, technology, Title III bilingual, and Title IV safety would tag along. We would send enough people to cover the whole building, while the other folks would focus on the Central Office. There usually would be a team of six to eight people on each visit. We would go into the schools and check to ensure the documents collected by the district could prove that the compliance requirements were present. This included documents, memos, and sign-in sheets, agendas, data reviews, and curriculum decisions. This often included checking for payroll certifications. Teachers just want to see their paychecks. We were now asking that they signed a document regularly indicating they were paid by federal monies.

We needed to check if the schools were providing services to poor students, so we visited classrooms to verify the presence of reading and math specialists. We talked to parents and teachers to make sure they were included in all federal money planning activities. Several parents had no idea how many rights the government tried to give them in educational operations for their schools. Schools had very little idea of what was required of them under federal regulations. For many administrators, the Consolidated Application is a duty as assigned. It is not a core function, but with all the regulations, laws, and requirements, it is easily a part-time job. I learned how limiting some of the federal requirements can be for districts to spend the money. It needs to be in addition to state and local funds. It cannot replace local funds. For several schools, especially in a recession period of 2007-2012, there were no more funds. The federal funds coming in were the difference between scraping by and closing up shop.

I felt so bad when we visited schools. I knew most of these folks from my visits during the year. They were busy and asked to do a lot. Most administrators were busier than the teachers, who had negotiated duty-free breaks and obligation-free lunches. One principal, very pregnant during one of my visits, started to cry when I told her secretary to hold all calls and asked her to eat lunch with me. She told me that she hadn't eaten lunch since becoming an Assistant Principal. Not cool. People have to eat. People cannot give 100% of the time all of the time. They will burn out.

So next time you think teaching is easy, remember: some teachers don't eat or use the restroom until after the students have left.

How do you avoid burnout as an educator?
#ThinkingAboutTeachingBook

PART II

CURRICULUM AND INSTRUCTION

MUSINGS, THOUGHTS, AND REFLECTIONS

In this next section, I look specifically at curriculum and instruction—the heart and soul of the teaching profession. I take you, the reader, with me through some everyday experiences to explore how to implement some really awesome adventures in the classroom. It is time to re-inspire our students in class. After all, there are so many ways to get excited about learning! In this day and age, our students have so many resources at their fingers, literally with smartphones and Google and new voice-activated devices, they can literally have the world at their voice command!

21. WATER AND FIRST WORLD ISSUES

*F*riday, we experienced a water main break, again. It happened again in our very suburban, very lovely area of Albany County. I went down to talk with the crew fixing the infrastructure and was told by a very hard-working member of the crew from the local Civil Service Employees Association (CSEA) that the average infrastructure for the town water system is over 50 years old and needs significant replacement. It got me thinking about water and the first-world problems associated with failing infrastructure.

Historical Significance of Water

From a historical perspective, civilization started near water valleys in the Indus, the Tigris and Euphrates, the Huang He, and in Central America. The Mississippi, Missouri, Hudson-

Mohawk, and the Susquehanna River valleys of North America, as well as the Five Great Lakes and the St. Lawrence, have become a significant route for transportation and farming. The Rio Grande and Colorado rivers in the West have been home to major native cultures throughout history.

Water is critical for transportation, potable drinking, farming, and food harvesting for fisheries. Humans need water and have used it for manufacturing, cooling, and power. The historical development of the U.S. is tied to water. The Niagara Falls Hydro Power project generates clean, renewable energy. Benjamin (2014) looked at the history of the Hudson Valley. This phenomenal book looks at the Revolution to the Civil War period. The Erie Canal, the Ohio River Valley, and the Mississippi have all supported floating goods to market. The water from creeks and the Hudson River powered Troy NY's Burden Iron Works-key to the Northern victory in the Civil War. The Erie Canal made cities in Buffalo, Rochester, and Syracuse.

In Europe, the **Hanseatic League** created a network of trading cities that were linked by the Baltic Sea. The rivers in Europe created a network for cities to communicate and trade along these routes. The ancient Roman Empire engineered a system to carry water from the hills and rivers to the cities of the empire to support the fountains, drinking needs, and sanitation needs of the metros of the period. The system of aqueducts still stands across Europe as a testament to the engineering abilities of the empire back in that era.

Before Rome, Petra in the Middle East transported water across the town. Residents in cities wanted clean water supplies. Dr. John Snow mapped Cholera in London (Tuthill, 2003). This example of a primary source document is useful for teachers who want to help explain the significance of water to a city.

Today, water is key to manufacturing. It needs to be clean, and it must meet the needs of companies creating products as far-ranging as sports drinks, wrenches, and energy. Manufacturing used water from rivers to power flour mills, weaving mills, and metalwork.

My Situation

When the water was out in my neighborhood, it was an inconvenience, yet it wasn't devastating. We had bottled water from the supermarket, and we still had a toilet. Our water is clean and usually runs from the tap on command. We don't need to walk miles to get water like people in sub-Saharan Africa. We aren't subjected to repeated Typhoid epidemics, and we don't suffer from drought-like is currently affecting large areas of the world. We are pretty blessed.

However, we do suffer from failing infrastructure, much of which needs to be replaced. For example, we lose too much potable water in aging infrastructure. We, as a nation, also need to look at returning to the wise use of water to generate more power, reducing our dependence on fossil fuels. For example, wave- and river-based power supplies should have enough energy to power cities and suburbs.

We also need to look at the oceans and lakes as treasures and not dumping grounds. Water quality is so important, not only in the Northeast where water is abundant, but everywhere. Water politics will probably be the next major conflict in the world.

Students engaged in Common Core exercises should research water in their own areas. Teachers guiding learners should discuss topics such as:

1. Water-based settlement patterns
2. Water pollution and remediation
3. Water service and sewage disposal costs
4. Water's influence on different areas across the globe.

An amazing project which students should think about undertaking is water quality research in their local neighborhoods and communities. For urban students, a tap or water fountain will do fine. In suburban areas, a quick trip to a park or preserve will help. For our rural areas, streams, lakes, and rivers, ponds are in abundance.

An ideal lesson plan would look like:

1. Find the standards which you are going to address. National, state, and local curriculum guides should

be the first place you start. Once you have identified your own standards area, team with another teacher for their standards area. For instance, water fits well with science, social studies, and math. English or Literature has several examples of how water has influenced people in their writing.

2. Once you have identified your standards, find your goal for the unit or lesson. What do you want students to do? Once you have identified the primary goal, begin to plan how you will assess the students to determine if they achieved the intent of the unit or lesson. Will you use a rubric to see if the students met the standard or mastery?

3. Once the assessment has been planned, begin to identify the activities students will undertake as they learn the process. For a water-based unit, let's examine an earth science/social studies/literature lesson.

4. The Mediterranean Basin: From a multi-disciplinary perspective, this area lends itself well to a thematic unit. In social studies, the students study the Mediterranean region for significant historical and geographical issues. Starting with the Ancient seafaring civilizations of the coasts, and moving into Alexander the Great, the Persians, the Romans, the Ottomans, the Spice Trade, and

multiple historical events, and the current day refugee crisis have impacted the region.

5. From a science perspective, the region suffers from tectonic activity, including volcanoes, earthquakes, and climate differentiation. The region has desert, lush waterways, and immense saline content.

6. From a literary perspective, multiple stories have been written concerning the Mediterranean Sea. This includes T*he Iliad, The Odyssey,* and *The Travels of Ibn Battuta* (Dunn, 2012; Manguel, 2009).

7. After the teams have established what activities the students will undertake, it will be time for the teams to select a wide range of sources. If your school is fortunate enough to have 1:1 laptop programs, students should be encouraged to use web-based sources. Some of the sources can include the following:

8. A map of the settlement patterns on the Mediterranean.

9. A seismic activity map, which includes earthquakes, volcanoes, and other geological activity.

10. A chart of exports, imports, and trade routes from the area.

11. Excerpts from primary source documents and literature from the region.

12. The teams of students in each class should be tasked with developing some variety of presentation/research project which demonstrates their abilities to meet the national, state, and local standards. This may include a plan to help assist refugee resettlement in the area, or a way to discuss how to ensure that historical treasures are made accessible to non-wealthy travelers.

The idea of working with everyday events and occurrences can help enliven the curriculum and make it more relevant for students. If we return back to the ideas of aquifers and the engineering of the 2000-year-old water systems and tie it in with the disaster that Flint, Michigan experienced with lead in its water, students can see that these are current, relevant, and troubling problems which aren't going away.

How do you provide authentic learning experiences?
#ThinkingAboutTeachingBook

22. IN PRAISE OF THE ENVIRONMENT

*W*atching the History or Discovery Channel, you might see programs about "the end of human civilization," or maybe "what would the world look like if humanity was gone." Well, we don't have to speculate. We can observe what happens to the Earth after humans vanish. We can look in war zones like the Korean Demilitarized zone, or in the Chernobyl disaster areas. We also have a third option in the USA, in New York State. In an effort to save some of the most environmentally sensitive lands in New York and preserve the water supply for New York City, the state's constitution adopted a "forever wild" provision (McMartin, 1992).

According to the New York State Constitution:

The lands of the state, now owned or hereafter acquired, constituting the forest preserve as now fixed by law, shall be forever kept as wild forest lands. They shall not be leased, sold or exchanged, or be taken by any corporation, public or private, nor shall the timber thereon be sold, removed or destroyed.

— NEW YORK STATE CONSTITUTION, 1895

New York, with several urban blighted areas and masses of suburban sprawl, created two of the largest forest preserves in the world, the Adirondacks and the Catskills. Granted, many wealthy NYC residents acquired large palatial camps in the Adirondacks (Reynolds, 2011), but to a large extent, the area is relatively untouched. There are parts of the Adirondacks where very few humans have ever seen a sun rise or set from the tops of the mountains. The lore of the park and the natural environment allows for a diverse set of flora and fauna. There are stands of old-growth trees and crystal clear lakes. You can hear the call of a loon, or see a beaver dam, almost as it was when the area was first explored.

For residents living inside of the Blue Line, or the boundaries of the park, restrictions may be overbearing. The limitations on economic activity, building activity, and other money-making ventures crimp the growth abilities of some communities. The NYS Rural Schools Center has data that indicates the counties within the Adirondacks have lost population (PAD

Cornell, ND). An article published by the Adirondack Almanac suggests that many school communities in the Park zone are losing population and seeking alternatives to school consolidation. Many of the countries suffer from an unemployment rate of around 6%. Six percent of Hamilton County's 4,000+ residents is equal to approximately 240 people without work. For an area that small, that number is enormous.

Tourism, resource extraction, and education are Hamilton County's largest employers. For educators and tourists, environmental preservation ranks high. For members of resource extraction, good stewardship of the natural resources ensures continued employment. The largest landowner in the county is the State Government. Most of this land is dedicated to preservation and outdoor recreation.

What is unique about the Adirondacks is the previous industrial aspect of the region. Many authors have addressed this. For example, Farrell (1995) wrote about the mining operations within the Park boundaries before the state constitution required the area to be preserved. McMartin (1992) examined the tanning industry in the region. Porter (2009) discussed the conservation efforts in the Adirondack Mountains in-depth. Allen et al. (1990) wrote a magnificent article about the Archaeology of the Bloomery forges in the Adirondacks. These sources describe different aspects of the park before it was saved as a "forever wild" place. The labor and resource-heavy industries in the region could have damaged some amazing areas permanently. Instead, the park areas recovered.

There are scholarships available to readers, historians, environmentalists, and people realistically seeking environmental recovery.

After the end of many intensive industries in the Adirondack, the area recovered, except for a brief time when acid rain from the Midwest began to pollute the lakes. Johnson, Andersen, and Siccama (1994) wrote a scientific paper that examined the phenomena and found that the side effects of deindustrialization in the Midwest one have been cleaner environments to the east. The decreasing level of pollution has helped the area to self-clean and allowed for the rehabilitation of smaller lakes and streams.

Now, the Adirondacks are facing an invasion of Zebra Mussels. Careless boaters, who do not realize how destructive practices such as a dirty boat or a filled bilge can ruin ecosystems, carry invasive species unknowingly into unaffected lakes and ponds with careless inattention to details. As the communities surrounding Lake George are worried about water quality, the state has instituted new mandatory actions for boaters entering the Park.

On a more personal note, I love the Adirondacks. My enjoyment started when I was young, and the family and Uncle Steve went to Lake Placid for a winter vacation. We saw the Olympic Park, and Dad and Uncle Steve went on the bobsled run. We saw the ski jumps and the village itself. When we lived in Gloversville, one of our favorite pastimes as a family involved swimming and picnic lunches at Great Sacandaga Lake. We would explore the Civilian Conservation Corps planted trees, all in straight rows, and swim and eat on the beach. It was quiet and relaxing. The CCC was a Great Depression-era project to employ young men to reforest the areas clear cut during industrialization. My godfather, Uncle Steve Kovack, was a true mountaineer and a member of the Adirondack Club. He climbed a number of the 46'ers or highest peaks in the park. Rest in peace, Uncle Steve. You are missed.

An amazing place for a family to visit, the region also boasts some of the best tourist destinations. This includes the Six Flags Great Escape in Queensbury/Lake George. The million-dollar beach in Lake George and the islands in the lake are amazing. There are several Six Years and Revolutionary forts in the region, including Fort George, Fort William Henry, Crown Point, and Fort Ticonderoga. In Plattsburgh, NY, just outside of the region lies the War of 1812 forts and historic sites. Within the Blue Line lies Enchanted Forest Water Safari and the Fulton Chain of lakes.

I visited the Old Forge/Town of Webb Central School District when interviewing for a principal position. On the drive up from the Utica side of the area, I passed Woodgate, NY, home to Camp Russell, and the site of fond memories from when I was Otahnagon Lodge's Associate Adviser. On the way home, I drove through Inlet, NY, a small school associated with Webb, but still independent. I passed Raquette Lake, a community that has a school and no children—

because they are tuitioned to neighboring schools. I passed Blue Mountain Lake. There is the Adirondack Museum and Experience—one of the most amazing small museums in NY. I also saw one of the BIGGEST herds of deer in my life, almost 30, as they ran across NY Route 28. I had no cell phone service, but I loved every minute of it.

As I drove south along Route 30, I passed Speculator, NY, and the only gas station for what seemed forever! Thank God for the people in that region. I passed through Wells and Northville, where a dear friend of mine from Grad School at State University of New York (SUNY) Albany started her administrative career. As I entered Gloversville and the New York State Thruway, I realized that the park shows the lonely part of society. It also shows the community side of life. Old Forge reaches some of the lowest temperatures in North America—yet the community is so well connected. The park shows not only the past in the decaying archaeology regions, and the small towns struggling to survive, but also the future. The schools in the region are collaborating as the True North Group, in an effort to offer their students the best any suburban school can. Newcomb Central School District, through the creative efforts of its superintendent, brought a school on the brink back to a mecca for international exchange programs (Winerip, 2011).

I challenge you—come visit New York Adirondack, and see the past, present, and future all within a gaze at the mountains.

Challenge

As teachers worry about the Common Core (National Governors Association, 2010), a suggestion for their class is to identify an at-risk property in their neighborhood and launch a
campaign to save it. Address letters to the editor, local political leaders, and develop public speaking points. Contact the
local records office and research the history that happened on
the property. You may find some amazing events and occurrences. Try having students organize a town hall meeting or a
public forum in conjunction with the local library.

As a teacher, think about how you would ask students to
research environmental issues. To what extent can you ask
inquiry-based questions about changes in the environment?
What sources or collaboration with earth science can you
brainstorm? I would start by exploring major locations thought
the US dedicated to land and water preservation. With my
seventh grade students, I focused quite a bit on the Adirondack
and Catskill Parks. These large state parks in New York are
huge. They encompass millions of acres of land. These two
regions form the "bumper" points for west-east travel in New
York State. The Mohawk River Valley is the only route that
allows people to move west to the Great Lakes. This is why
the Erie Canal was built along the river and continued on west
to Lake Erie.

I would then ask my seventh graders to discuss how the
canal and the industry along the Hudson River impacted the

environment and the communities which surrounded the waterways. We, as a class, investigated how power was harnessed by people and used to raise and lower boats along the Canal. We searched out ways that the areas in the Adirondacks and the Catskills were preserved, while the river center was developed. If we as teachers take the time to make the local relevant, then our students will see the connection to their daily lives.

What local landmarks are a must-see, concerning your chosen content area?

#ThinkingAboutTeachingBook

23. MICROHISTORY AND GUARDIANS

*I*n grad school, I wrote a paper about the Iroquois Influence Debate that pitted the biggest names in the historical profession against Don Grinde and Bruce Johansen. Grinde and Johansen are two academics who were not part of the traditional historical world. They specialized in communications studies and anthropology. There were miles of ink spilled in the debate between those who believed that the Iroquois influenced the creation of the American Constitution and those who took a more traditional approach. The traditional approach believed American Constitutional thoughts emerged out of English Law and Ancient Greek and Roman legal traditions.

Essentially, Grinde and Johansen argued separately and together that the Iroquois influenced the American constitution. Their thesis stated, in summary, that the Iroquois governing structure of a "republic" made the American colonists realize that a less centralized government was a great idea (Johansen & Grinde, 1990). After this thesis and articles came out, a series of scathing attacks were made against Grinde and Johansen. The historical profession took to task every aspect of their writing, from the evidence they used to the places they published, to the assumptions that were made by the authors. It was a really in-depth process by the historical world to justify why the accepted "Roman influence" thesis was not only more correct, but the only correct interpretation (Levy, 1996).

I have recently become concerned with what I see as the movement of the many to disagree and discount the experiences of the few in the "authentic" record. We have seen a significant number of quotes about "alternative facts appearing." I want to take a moment and think through alternative facts and the living reality of the few.

In many ways, history is written by the majority. It is written by consensus among the historical field based upon the sources which were left during the time. It takes a significant amount of peer review before theories pass muster and enter into accepted historical understanding and "cannon." And yet, as the movie *Minority Report* (Molen, 2002) reminds us, there are always those who disagree. In the movie, a person is accused of a pre-crime and is hunted down to prevent the crime from occurring. There is no get out of jail free. When one of the officers charged with enforcing the law is accused of a pre-crime, he finds out that there is no unanimous agreement in the prediction of the pre-crime. Instead, a "minority report" may indicate that the crime might not be committed.

In history, we have these "minority reports." Some historians often buck the trend, find a different interpretation, and publish alternative views on events. Many times, these historians do not gain fame, or prestige, or that rarest of jobs: tenure-track positions. It often takes decades for these views or facts to become considered in the mainstream of the historical canon.

Women, people of color, and gender-nonconforming people (which will include LGBTQ members of society) were frequently excluded from the historical record in the past. If not for the works of Mary Beth Norton, Gary Nash, or John Hope Franklin, this rich, engaging, and essential part of the American narrative would not have gained its place in the canon of history. The three authors I listed are experts in the areas of history, which describes the contribution of women and underrepresented populations as central to their roles. I would encourage all historians, students of history, and social studies teachers to think about how we encourage our students to examine their histories, but more importantly, the microhistories which add depth and breadth to the historical narrative. Ask students to take time and compare the historical narrative about the first Persian Gulf War with their parents, grandparents, aunts, and uncles, and what is written in their history textbook. Then compare the narrative in different textbooks written by different authors. A really great, advanced experience is to explore textbooks written in Canada, England, or Australia. How is the first Persian Gulf War covered in other nations' histories?

History and the way we remember history can be deceiving. It may not focus on those people who contributed at a local level, or at an industrial scale. History is often taught as a grand narrative, and the "little people" are forgotten as class time covers the "great leader" and ignores the role everyday people played.

What is microhistory? Essentially, it is history at the smallest levels. It is not referenced in the work by Bernard Bailyn (2011) or Jared Diamond (1998). These two authors represent sweeping macro history, examining history on a grand scale. Both have written works about the mass movements of people and civilization. I prefer microhistory instead. It is local, it is singular, and it is personal. Alfred Young (1999) does a fantastic job in his work, *The Shoemaker and the Tea Party,* in exploring the microhistory of the Boston Tea Party. Maybe reading about Clara Barton would be a good start. Who was Clara? She founded the American Red Cross. This one individual changed the world profoundly: creating a caring organization. I, for one, love the new book *Hidden Figures* (Shetterly, 2016) about the role of women in NASA. This well-written work examines a forgotten and essential STEM area that gives young people some role models.

Since I am writing this chapter on Mother's Day, I would

be remiss if I did not mention my mom, Patricia Jakubowski, who serves as a great story of her own. Born in South Buffalo to a poor German and Irish family whose members had served as firefighters and mechanics, my mother gave up her dream of oceanography to become a nurse. Graduating from E.J. Meyer School of Nursing in Buffalo, Mom served as a nurse at Buffalo General, then went on to work at Nathan Littauer Hospital in Gloversville. Mom also served as a nurse for Our Lady of Victory home for children in Lackawanna, NY, and as a state nursing home/safety inspector and a psych hospital nurse. Mom has always helped those in need—friends of the family, family members, or children whose own parents could not or would not help them. Mom has taken the nursing oath:

> *Before God and those assembled here, I solemnly*
>   *pledge;*
> *To adhere to the code of ethics of the nursing*
>   *profession;*
> *To cooperate faithfully with the other members of the*
>   *nursing team and to carryout [sic] faithfully and to*
>   *the best of my ability the instructions of the*
>   *physician or the nurse who may be assigned to*
>   *supervise my work;*
> *I will not do anything evil or malicious and I will not*
>   *knowingly give any harmful drug or assist in*
>   *malpractice.*

I will not reveal any confidential information that may
come to my knowledge in the course of my work.
And I pledge myself to do all in my power to raise the
standards and prestige of the practical nursing
May my life be devoted to service and to the high
ideals of the nursing profession.

— AMERICAN NURSES ASSOCIATION, 2001

AS A SOCIETY, WE MUST NO LONGER IGNORE THE "MINORITY reports" from the past. Our country is changing. We cannot white-wash history. Ethically, teachers need to ensure space is given to students to find their own stories. The classroom must be a place of orchestra music. Each instrument supports the fantastic sound of every other one. They often don't play the same notes, but to an audience, there is harmony. Part of this is ethics. Teach your students ethics, for no other reason than ethical thinking and deci-sion-making, is the ground to which civil society is based. It was extremely unethical for researchers in the past to ignore groups that contributed so much. Maybe we need to take a page from the medical profession and, as teachers, swear an oath in public to act and be ethical and inclusive. Spend time allowing students to research people who have great stories to tell, but have been passed over. Use your platform for social justice and change.

How can you, as a classroom teacher, do this? Interviews are great ways to begin the process. Work with a local senior citizens center to start interviewing the residents or the clients. Ask students to tell the story of a resident. They need to do the following:

- Ask permission from the school and the senior citizens center to have the students and residents participate in these interviews.
- Have students write letters introducing themselves to the residents and why they are undertaking the project. Tell the residents what they can expect in terms of length of time.
- Have the students review how to conduct an interview and how to behave. Have the students practice interviewing skills and questions within English class.
- Have the students write out five open-ended questions to ask a resident. Teach the students how to ask follow-up questions.
- Record the interviews. Contact the local historical society and let them know these interviews were conducted and ask for the materials to be placed in the collection.
- Have the students turn the interviews into a "This Is Your Life" poster or presentation and deliver the

findings to friends, families, residents, and community members.

This is just one way to save the memories and the life experiences of people who have influenced your local community. With the increasing interest in genealogy and local history, future researchers will appreciate your efforts. Family members of residents in the senior center will appreciate your interest in their family members—and the residents really like interacting with students!

What are some ways to be intentional about presenting a balanced view of history? **#ThinkingAboutTeachingBook**

24. REFLECTION ON THE FOURTH OF JULY

"Far, we've been traveling far..." opens Neil Diamond's song "America" (Diamond et al., 2005). I think about this weekend because it reminds me of my family and the purpose of America. On a personal level, my mother is celebrating her birthday. She is my guiding strength and one of the greatest people I know. Mom was born into a working-class family that had provided service to our nation in war and peace. She graduated from South Park High School. It was a rough part of South Buffalo, an Irish neighborhood. She grew up strong.

For her profession, my mom became a nurse, graduating from EG Meyer's School of Nursing (now UB Nursing). She went to work caring for the neediest. One of the positions she held was working with children who had been abandoned by their families. Mom treated them as if they were part of her family. Reflecting the work of The Venerable Father Nelson Baker, my mother has always had a way of helping those in need. Later, my mother went to work for the State, serving as a nurse at the Buffalo Psych Center. There, she provided comfort to those who needed help soothing the demons of their minds. As part of her work, Mom saw to the safety and health of public workers throughout Western New York, such as the Corrections Officers at a corrections facility. She also ensured teachers were safe from harm at schools. She helped volunteer firefighters be safe during their vigilance. Before she retired from the state, Mom served as a nursing home inspector. There she had a responsibility to ensure the elderly who were most at risk were cared for compassionately, correctly, and competently by the medical staff.

My mother, born into a working-class family in a poor area of South Buffalo, NY, rose above this to ensure people most in need of protection because they protected others had the support. My mother is my hero. She is a great person. I truly love her.

JULY 3 IS MY PARENT'S WEDDING ANNIVERSARY. MARRIED IN the1970s, they met in a hospital, where my Dad had suffered from an accident caused by a drunk driver. Mom nursed him back to health. My father overcame some significant injuries to court my mother, as well as to finish his degree in Chemistry from University at Buffalo. Dad's family came from Poland and were farmers, who had worked on the railroad. He then worked as a railroad fireman. Dad's work on the railroad allowed him to travel but caused him to miss a very brief time when we were growing up. Dad made up for that later in life, as he became our Scout Leader in Cub and served as our troop committee Chairman. Dad took us camping to Canada, Gettysburg, the National Jamboree, and Philmont. His service in scouting was also part of his work during the day. Dad served first as a chemist in the Department of Environmental Conservation (DEC), ensuring water quality at the Great Sacandaga Lake in the Adirondacks. After DEC protection, my dad went to work at the Asbestos Control Bureau in Buffalo. Rising to the ranks of a regional supervisor, Dad ensured that workers, citizens, and community members were safe from asbestos when it was present, and made sure that it was removed. Dad worked hard and was dedicated to making sure companies did what was right and safe. In the span of five generations, our family had gone to college and had served the community.

My parents inspired our family to serve the community. My sister, Emily, works with researchers in medical efforts to help people. My brother, Nick, works with technology at a college in the Buffalo region. I worked at the State Department of Education to help students improve.

On July 4th, let us not just have a picnic and watch parades. Remember why the United States of America came into being: we are a land of opportunity for people looking for a second start. America welcomes people who are "tired, poor, huddled masses yearning to breathe free..." (Lazarus, 2002).

We should not go back to the days of hatred, discrimination, and imperialism. Citizens of America are great people. Let's dedicate ourselves to service projects, helping our neighbors, and improving the lives of the weakest and neediest.

On a personal note, to quote Outkast (2003): "*Thank God for Mom and Dad* For *sticking through together*. Cause we don't know how...." You are role models for Nick, Marissa, Emily, Elizabeth, and me.

Lesson Connection

Now that I have told you a little about my family, how would you ask your students to connect these dots?

First, have the students pick a holiday that is part and parcel of their family. Is it a national holiday, or a family event? Have the students interview their families to see how the event evolved. How did their parents get to this point in their lives?

Second, ask students to brainstorm ways their family makes an impact on the local community. How do their jobs or service work, or hobbies or interests help inspire those around the area to do better? Is there an area that would lack attention if their families didn't help out?

Third, have students interview an older relative or neighbor or friend of the family. How has that person seen the changing area during their lifetime? Were they surprised by anything which developed or did not develop? Does the friend or family member know where the family came from? Can they trace their family back in time?

Fourth, have the students try and make connections with their classmates. Are they connected via family, friends, activities, interests, or events? How many interconnections occur among the class? Develop a visual presentation for a talk or an open house.

Fifth, have students talk to a career counselor about what interests them. How could the career impact society, and how could, as a young person, this career get started in the immediate school year?

What were the major takeaways your students had after completing the activity?
#ThinkingAboutTeachingBook

25. ELECTION OF 2016

*C*an I ask a question to my friends who teach social studies? How do we feel about the 2016 U.S. presidential election? Not about who won or lost. Not about the *politics of the election*, but about how people do not actually understand a lot of the concepts we taught in class? I say, "we," because I know I taught it. I remember going over in seventh, eleventh, and twelfth grades the basics of elections at the national level. I remember discussing the Electoral College. I remember discussing the need to respect every person, even if their opinions disagreed with our own. I remember reviewing the old New York State Standards for social studies, where we talked about geography and economics and history. Later, working for the State Department of Education, I remember reviewing the new social studies frameworks, the ones the Content Advisory Panel, and I helped to create.

Reviewing the run-up, election, and post-election has caused me to want to reflect on a 15-year career in education. We teach quite a bit about the electoral process in New York State. In fact, it is part of seventh, eleventh, and twelfth-grade Participation in Government courses. Students who graduate from a New York State school have been at least exposed to the process. In the 2016 post-election hubbub, many people were confused about the presidential election process. They were bewildered: "she won the popular vote, *but lost the election?!? How often has this happened?!?"*

There have been other times that I have run into a situation when intelligent people don't remember or understand a logical point about history, or government, or economics.

Let's mention geography for a minute. I love geography. I love historical geography. I love maps. As a kid, I used to pull out and study the National Geography maps. As a teacher, I was obsessed with making sure students had maps and used them. As a kid, I loved using maps in Boy Scouts and understanding the keys and the meanings of the legend. On a family vacation to Chicago, I helped navigate us from the suburban hotel to the Museums of Science and Industry.

Everywhere we went as a family, and now as an adult, I use maps and alternative paths to reach my destination. Google Maps are fun, but I think I can do a better job of navigating than a GPS unit (or so I think!). But so many people I know do not understand how to navigate with maps. I have never once tried to drive my car into a river! Many students hated the map questions on the Regents exams. Granted, the black and white doesn't help, and I have long advocated that Students with Disabilities (SWDs) taking the exam to be given colored copies. Now with computer-based testing in NY (Amin, 2019), I hope the maps are colored.

My classes were challenged to explore information in maps. Maybe I failed, personally, as an instructor in communicating critical points to my past students. Perhaps there is too much info to learn in social studies. Bain (2004), in his book *What the Best College Teachers Do,* describes the reality that good college teachers often feel like failures if their students did not do well. After the election, I felt that my time in the classroom was for naught. Many American citizens do not understand the foundations of our democracy. This is disconcerting, to say the least.

As a member of the Capital District Council for the Social Studies, a former New York State Council for the Social Studies and National Council for Social Studies (NCSS)/Council University Faculty Association organizations, I am pleading with my fellow teachers to dig deep and reflect on how we teach participation. With election turnouts in primaries at very low levels (Green & Gerber, 2015) and almost 45% of eligible voters not voting (Regan, 2016), something is failing us.

Americans want to participate...we like to participate. We

will respond to web polls, Facebook, and SurveyMonkey polls. We will vote for an Idol (Sweney, 2006) and someone who has talent, but we don't like to vote for our leaders. How do we drive that participation? How do we make voting a sacred duty, one that our founders and our service people fought and died to give us?

I voted. I voted out of a sense of duty. I voted out of an obligation. I voted because I wanted the right to participate in the process. I voted because my paternal great-grandfather wanted to do his duty during World War I, but couldn't because he had just immigrated. I voted in honor of my grand-fathers and great uncles who fought in World War II. I voted in honor of my in-law uncle, who served in Vietnam. I voted in honor of Scouter Bill Wisniewski, who fought in Vietnam. He was the scoutmaster who welcomed me into my Boy Scout troop. He later died after stomach cancer robbed him of the last 25 years of his life. I voted in honor of my students, my friends, my classmates who served and continue to serve in US action in the Middle East, Afghanistan, and around the world. I voted in honor of my brother-in-law, an Iraqi vet. I voted in honor of Isaac Nievies, one of my students from Sidney, who lost his life in Iraq.

How do we instill a sense of pride, of honor, of duty, of deeply caring? How do we explain difficult concepts to understand?

One such resource is the NCSS. There are a ton of resources on the organization's website. The resources include how to teach voting. The lessons include information on how voting patterns emerged over many of the elections. The work provides information on how to run elections. Use those resources. Use resources from your League of Women Voters. Go to Rock the Vote webpages.

Do whatever it takes to inspire students to become active in civic engagement and participation. Let's make an effort to improve civic literacy as New York Chancellor of the Board of Regents has stated is so essential (Rosa, 2016). Civic literacy is the foundation of understanding how democracy and government work. The leader of the third-largest state in the union and home to the largest city has unequivocally stated that we must teach the foundation of our government to the next generation and beyond.

Lesson Idea on Civic Literacy

The first step for this lesson idea is to start with the civics section of your state's standards. Ask yourself what you want to achieve with your students in the area of civic literacy. Usually, a local civic issue is a great place to start with your students. Invite a local civic representative to discuss how local laws are created in the students' hometowns.

Your second step is to design a project that engages the students in some level of activity, which explores an issue in depth. Researching and writing a report is really not a great idea—instead, ask the students how social media on an issue and the use of GoFundMe and personal connections are driving engagement.

A third step in the lesson is to ask students to create a tangible product that will help educate the public about a single student or team's viewpoints on a topic of debate locally. Have these items displayed or presented at an evening activity and invite the community. This is especially relevant during election season.

What were the major takeaways your students had after completing the activity? **#ThinkingAboutTeachingBook**

26. THE COLD OF WINTER

*A*s many of you in education (particularly those who live in areas where it snows) know, the cold of winter is a tough time to teach and learn. The days are short. The dark is long. We wake up and go into school early before the sun has risen. We leave the building at 4 PM, and the sun is setting. We go from a warm bed to a cold car, to a crazy temperature building where it is either too hot or too cold. And then we go home, starting our journey in a cold car, on ice or snow-covered roads. We arrive home and have snow in the driveway. Let us also not forget about the germs, viruses, and bacteria wandering around our petri dish classrooms of children. Runny noses, unwashed hands, coughs, sneezes, and occasionally other bodily functions let loose as some sort of bug infects us. And if we are so blessed to have children at home, we have yet another differing set of bugs!

Question: have you thought about using the cold and the germs as teaching tools? There are two great books out there, which can help us capture students' attention and understand how the climate and the micro-fauna impacted history. Let's start with the cold.

Brian Fagan's (2000) *The Little Ice Age* explores how the world, especially Europe, was impacted by a precipitous drop in temperature in the 1300-1800s. This is an easy read for many students in grade nine and up. The author makes the history of climate accessible and exciting. By using anecdotes from people's lives of the period, we are captured as readers in the drama of day-to-day life. For instance, one chapter, "The Summer that Wasn't," portrays the depth of climate impact on the farmers, villagers, and merchants who lived through the coldest, wettest period of European climate on record. The book ties in well with earth science classes for high school students, so they can see how weather and climate affect people's daily lives. In the national social studies standards (NCSS, 2014), geography and its influence on people is one of the ten themes that the Council recommends all students learn. In my home state of New York, the importance of geography on people is a near-guaranteed question on the Regents Exam.

Reading excerpts from texts and other books, as well as articles, are critical to helping students see how climate has influenced history. The classroom-based discussions that teachers could implement should then broaden into how climate patterns are now impacting people, starting with the Dust Bowl in the 1920s and how the United States, specifically California, was impacted in the late 2010s. Next, the class could discuss how air conditioning made living in the south more tenable, and conclude by examining how the Great Lakes and its weather patterns impact New York, Ohio, Pennsylvania, and Michigan. In the winter, cold winds blowing over open lake water generate large snowstorms called lake effect storms. These storms blow feet of snow onto the land and dramatically impact conditions in cities along the lakes. In 1977, Buffalo was affected by such a snowstorm, which is famous up to the present.

My home city, Buffalo, NY, has great ski country because of the Lake Effect snows. The ski resorts have helped rebuild Ellicottville, NY,_from a sleepy village to a vibrant area. In 1998, there was one small supermarket and the ski hill in the village. Now, there are several shops, festivals, and attractions in the area. The craft beer brewing industry has helped make the area a destination outside of winter skiing. The Adirondacks and Catskills also have several winter weather venues. As the United States is moving away from resource extraction to an economy based on knowledge and the service sector, weather and climate will impact local areas more intensely than in the past (Florida, 2014). People will want to live in environmentally sustainable cities. People will want more, not less small scale "craft" and handmade products.

Lesson Ideas

Think about how you, as a teacher, would work with your students to examine the concept of cold, especially environmental cold. How does cold, even in a place like a desert, impact the residents? For me, I would:

1. Identify a major region of the world that has cold weather.

2. Identify the people who live in the area and how their culture accepts or actively works against the cold. To what extent does the cold expand what the region can do, or limit what the region can do?

3. Compare this region with a separate region. Do the two areas have significant overlap? Do they have significant differences? If this material is presented in a graphically appealing way, would someone understand what you are comparing and contrasting?

4. As a young person interested in DOING SOMETHING, think of a new way to deal with the cold in your area (if applicable). Design and sketch out this idea. Then, using materials you found, not purchased, build, and present this to your class.

What were the major takeaways your students had after completing the activity? **#ThinkingAboutTeachingBook**

27. GERMS AND YUCKIES

he book *Guns, Germs, and Steel* (Diamond, 1998) examines world history from the perspective of case studies. Its in-depth look at a variety of significant changes in world history as technology advanced (or failed to advance) is an excellent introduction for readers at the high school level. This book really digs into technology, its influence on people in various locations, and how their cultures reacted, deciding whether or not to adopt that technology. The book is readable and engaging for students who may not see social studies as engaging or interesting.

Let's start with germs. Diamond explains how germs really remade the world. Native people did not have immunity to the common cold virus, smallpox, or other communicable diseases. To Europeans, these germs were common childhood illnesses. Germs are fantastic for high school students to examine. In health and science classes, teachers are looking at a multitude of diseases. How do you prevent the flu? Wash your hands! How do you be safe with a partner? Use protection! In science classes, students learn about bacteria and viruses. As students in this age range are in school, they acquire acne, have wisdom teeth out, and are potentially exposed to meningitis from shared beverages or kissing! Why not use science, tech, history (health!) to discuss how diseases remade the world, why great Native American areas were wiped out, and how really unethical it was for the Sullivan campaign to use smallpox blankets in the American revolution.

A second lesson area is steel, which is a code word for technology. Our students don't really see how the evolution of hard metals has made a real difference in the current American lifestyle. In fact, in Earth Science class, students learn about the Mohs scale of hardness. It is time for the three areas to unite! The Earth Science teacher, the Social Studies teacher, and the Tech teacher need to work as a group to help students do some major lab experimenting! Start out this unit by conducting experimental archaeology.

Step 1: Identify three major tasks a person needs to carry out in a craft or a trade.
Step 2: Identify the materials required to undertake these tasks.

Step 3: Research the evolution of these tasks over 4,000 years.

Step 4: Design an experiment that would compare three sets of historically replicated tools to conduct this experiment.

Step 5: Engage in building these tools and demonstrate how you used these tools to create your experiment.

Step 6: Collect data and offer a report to the class and community.

Talc is the softest mineral known to humanity. A diamond is the hardest. The Mohs scale (Dixon, 1992) allows students to test and identify minerals by their hardness. But then what? What do you actually do with these materials? Mica is excellent as a countertop but can also be etched to make a computer chip. Which is better to split a log: wooden mallets, stone axes, or metal axes? As educators, our goal, our mission, our reason needs to revolve around teaching students how to ask great questions. If we are successful in teaching students how to ask great questions, then our efforts will help launch a generation into the wide world of critical thinking and research by asking amazing questions!

What were the major takeaways your students had after completing the activity? **#ThinkingAboutTeachingBook**

28. CIVIC ENGAGEMENT AND KNOPE

*M*any Social Studies teachers are nerds. We love being nerds. We love watching tv programs that are nerdy. Yet we hold one of the greatest responsibilities in the education world: to teach our children civic engagement. Recent reports in the 2010s have indicated that many people feel disengaged from civic society (Green & Gerber, 2015; Reagan, 2016). They feel left out. They feel like their voice is not heard. People think the government does not listen to the little guy and their issues. We have clearly had a miscommunication or a colossal failure to communicate.

Having taught senior year civics for almost five years and overseen a massive urban school district program in civics, as well as worked at the NYS education department in implementing state civics education, I can assure you—in the C3 and NYS civics standards, it is there. Does the education system discourage engagement by teaching in high school academically focused civic engagement as writing a paper instead of working on a cause?

These senior year students, many of whom are 17 or 18, are not sure how this class relates to basics like voter registration, or paying taxes, or registering for selective service. Many others are confused about how to interact with the local court's system if they are ticketed for speeding. What is worse, we never teach the basics of how to obtain a marriage license, or where to go if you have an issue with a building permit, or how to buy a house. We don't discuss what to do if there is an animal loose or how to obtain a dog license for a pet. We never discuss what local resources are available for our residents and citizens to use. As a school, we assume that the parents have done that. We have epically and completely failed our students to the point that many only feel comfortable interacting online and in virtual reality.

Thankfully, some of our political leaders are creating a movement and excitement in young voters. Former President Obama and former candidates Jill Stein have led mass engagements in politics and civics by young people. From their slogans to their platforms, to their social media and communication savvy, these leaders are asking our students to engage and to make the world better. It's almost as if JFK's call for the Peace Corps and AmeriCorps has found another generation that wants to go good for the sake of doing good. Some of this civic-mindedness is finding its way into Teach for America

(TFA). While maybe not the best way to engage in teaching, the TFA teachers are recruited from our best and brightest and serve in some of the most demanding schools. Not always successful, some of these TFAers still have something that regular educators are missing: social networks (Straubhaar & Gottfried, 2016).

See, I went to school at a State school. I am very proud of that education. I have not, nor have any of my classmates from high school, made enough money or become powerful enough to really make a significant difference outside of our own little worlds. The two most influential members of my high school class are an assistant superintendent and a high school principal. Classes behind me have people who are small business owners, and doctors and lawyers, but no one who you read about in *The New York Times* or *The Wall Street Journal*.

I applaud the work that many beginning teachers do, but we have to help these members of education gain the connection into networked environments. As research is beginning to show, being connected to wealth is one of the only solid ways to get change in education (Hess, 2005).

This brings me to Knope, or Leslie Knope, Amy Pohler's character on *Parks and Recreation* (Shenk, 2019). Leslie was an idealist, a public servant who wanted to do good work. Her seven-season arc takes her from the role of Deputy Director of Pawnee, Indiana parks and recreation department to a high-level job in national politics. The stories, while trite, or conflated, or farcical, do explain several civic engagement concepts in a way that is not dry or boring.

What does Leslie try to do? She wants to build a park. Leslie wants to create a beautiful area for the citizens of her city. Over the space of the series, you see Leslie working with different characters in her office who help, oppose, or frustrate her. She deals with state intervention and government shutdown. She deals with a public that does not always know what is good for it. At public hearings, her ideas are opposed by people for reasons which have nothing to do with creating a better place. When Leslie decides to run for office, the campaign deals with money, manipulation, and public distrust. Once elected to City council, she must work with people who are out to harm her efforts. Leslie deals with a log rolling incident where her "Fun in the Sun" legislation is held up to allow a councilman to get her office. When she tries to impose a sugar tax, the community hates her because they want their food, and the business world attacks and threatens to destroy her. A group demands her recall and are successful, even after she saves two cities. The groups call her a nag and a nanny.

Two examples of civic engagement in this vignette, teaching, and public service, are becoming increasingly overlooked as a route to return community investment. Young people want to volunteer, but don't know how. Civic engagement requires schools to teach students how to advocate and how to work to change the system. Spending a season as a member of the local parks department can be one way to engage and give back to your community. Teaching with TFA is another. Our civic world needs help.

As teachers, we need to be brave and talk to our students about civics. It is interesting to see this humorous comedy have so many situations that allow social studies teachers to look at and teach civics in depth. It shows the difficulties faced by women in a world with many male tendencies. The show examines small-town life from a less than flattering angle. It does provide many compelling female characters. It allows a grander discussion in its last season about corporate responsibility, the role of big data in our lives, and how we as citizens look to technology and trend makers for silly reasons. This show can help teachers discuss civic, economic, political, and other current issues in a funny but engaging way. Look into the show, and see what you think.

What other connections from media can you bring into your classroom? **#ThinkingAboutTeachingBook**

29. REENACTORS AND THEIR RELEVANCE

*W*hy do some kids find history so dull, and others can't wait to go to a museum or attend a living history day? Why have people in the U.S. started to find craft-based products more tolerable than mass-produced goods (Ocejo, 2017)?

My wife and I love living history! She enjoys crafting and sewing. She loves to work on period pieces. We both love finding out about what life was like in the past. We watched the entire *Time Team* series from the BBC (Lewis, Harding, & Aston, 2000). We both watched the Farming Series from BBC. I enjoy the museum, which is part of New York State's cultural heritage. Some of the museums include the Genesee Country Museum, the Buffalo Niagara Historic Village, and the Old Bethpage Village on Long Island. My wife grew up next to Museum Village in Orange County, NY. Her brother served as a Civil War Reenactor. One of my favorite social studies teachers in junior high was a Civil War Reenactor. A colleague of mine and a fellow Alpha Phi Omega member participates in Civil War Reenactment. There is a vast number of suppliers for re-enactment, including Townsend, Old Suttler's John, and Pearsons.

So why do people re-enact? For some, it's the process of studying archaeology and history by doing it through the process of experimental archaeology, a recognized field of study which allows scholars to glean an understanding into how tools were used, how structures were built, and how the daily lives of people came to be. Many times, the people involved in experimental archaeology provide valuable insight into how theory became applied practice. Other members of the community enjoy the fellowship of the community. They find the events and the comrades they make to be supportive and welcoming, and unique environment to pursue a passion (Rudolph, 2019).

There are websites, books, and a wide variety of YouTube videos devoted to the periods and materials for reenactment. If you want to learn how to cook from the Civil War era, there are recipes and cooking demos. Cookbooks abound. Different crafters make reproduction tools and equipment that would be used in the period. We all know food is a great attraction for people. From eating hardtack and salt pork to cakes and fry bread and roasts common to the era, a veritable feast can be consumed on a reenactment event weekend. One of my dear friends, Amelia, is involved with the SCA. Her mundane existence as a technology director at a school support system and her weekend persona are amazing in their existence. She is a thrown weapons master, and arts and crafts guru, and yet runs the website! It allows her enjoyment, fellowship, and acquisition in the knowledge of crafting skills that are dying. I would recommend each person look at the following books for understanding about re-enactors and craft skills:

Masters of Craft: Old Jobs in the New Urban Economy (Ocejo, 2017)

Reliving the Civil War (Hadden, 1999)

A Compendium of Common Knowledge, 1558-1603: Elizabethan Commonplaces for Writers, Actors & Re-enactors (Secara, 2008)

The Constructed Past: Experimental Archaeology, Education, and the Public (One World Archaeology) (Planel & Stone, 2003)

Bushcraft 101: A Field Guide to the Art of Wilderness Survival (Canterbury, 2014)

Popular media also discusses reenactors as well. Almost all of the series are BBC or CBC based television programming. Major news magazines like *Salon* and *The Atlantic* have run stories on reenactors, or living histories. Parks and Recreation had a historical reenactor as part of their series. NCIS used a re-enactor death to create a storyline. Bones has used historical re-enactors to advance the crime-fighting adventures of Dr. Brennan and Agent Booth.

One of my friends from western New York collaborates in a War of 1812 reenactment with Canadian units. This activity inspired him to study history at college. He also became part of a Reenactment club that started a Venturing Scout program on living history.

For students and adults, the living history world is a novel opportunity to wonder about what was. Our museums and historical societies do wonderful events, activities, and fairs that bring history alive. While not always 100% accurate, it does get the ball rolling. Just like genealogists and history written for the masses are not always accepted, historians and social studies teachers should look for common allies in our fight to be relevant and expose more students to the wonders of the past and the unique and gripping stories. Engagement = interest = relevance.

So how can you, as a classroom teacher, think about using re-enactment in your classroom to inspire learners to learn more? First: no guns! Let's just set that one right out in the open! Most schools have a no firearms policy. Additionally, the weaponry can cause discomfort in members of your classes who have experienced violence in the past. As educators, we need to ensure we provide safe spaces for our students, and the safe space should include no weaponry. Speak to your local museums about the displays or collections which exist in their control. Also, let's look at how to do some amazing things in the classroom on the domestic side. This exercise could be a great time to examine some interdisciplinary activities in your career education field, science field, math field, and literacy field.

First: Identify diaries/documents which describe the daily life of a person from the period. Have the students read the diaries and develop a "day in the life" schedule of a person from a wide variety of backgrounds and occupations.

Second: Have the students identify tasks that they want to research/experience as that person for the day. Ask the students to research the task and make a plan as to the following:

1. What was the task? Describe it in as many steps as possible.
2. What tool or tools did the person need to accomplish the task? Was it a solo exercise, or did it require a team?
3. How would the individual get the tools necessary to accomplish the task? How can your students build the tools?
4. What did the person wear? How can you create a costume of the individual from the period to wear while attempting the task?
5. What did the person eat? How do the meals differ

from meals served today? How did the ingredients and cooking methods differ?

6. Have the students keep a log as they make observations of how the daily tasks of work and meals evolved. Explain the scientific method, the capturing of data, and how observation and data collection can be used in evaluating a hypothesis.

7. Ask the science teacher to identify different types of raw materials available in the area, such as wood, minerals, metals, foods, and plants. Ask the students and the science teacher to research and report on how the area has changed in the last 50 or so years.

8. Ask home and careers teachers to help with the sewing, cooking, and other home-based activities, and have the students compare these activities with today's methods. If you do not have access to home and careers, contact your friendly neighborhood restaurants or civic centers for help. Some school districts may have non-credit adult extension education classes teaching cooking.

9. Ask tech teachers to help experiment with building tools and using the tools to create the products which the people under study made and used. If you do not have access to tech teachers, speak with local contractors or local construction businesses.

You are working on accomplishing a real-life study of the past. More importantly, you are asking students to see how technology's evolution has impacted their lives via experimentation. This attempt to recreate living history is one way to have students see themselves as maturing into responsible adults. Children of the past were asked to perform adult work much sooner than our dragged-out adolescence of today. By adult work, I mean metalworking, tanning, farm labor, and other craft-based labor. Help students see the past as an evolution of the present.

What were the major takeaways your students had after completing the activity? **#ThinkingAboutTeachingBook**

30. FINDING COLLECTIONS FOR LOCAL HISTORY

*O*ne primary requirement from the Common Core and a general best practice in education is the use of authentic sources in the classroom. Locally in New York State, we have several dedicated archives, museums, and libraries which are perfect for exploration and utilization. There are so many different locations and archives across the state which people can use.

The first area in the west is the Fenton Historical Museum in Chautauqua County, New York (www. fentonhistorycenter.org). This museum holds several collections that a student, a scholar, and, most notably, researchers and teachers would be interested in interrogating for classroom materials and research topics. The west was a significant part of the state's history, and the collections range from a

Supreme Court Justice who tried war criminals after World War II. The region is home to the SUNY Fredonia local history archives, and that organization contains several documents relating to the earliest settlers in the Holland Land Company region.

The second area for research is the Rochester community, specifically the film museum in George Eastman's home (www.eastman.org). This is a fantastic archive that allows researchers, scholars, and teachers the opportunity to examine one of the most significant collections of film in the Western world. The Eastman house also provides students the chance to see how a communication medium has evolved over the past 100 years from a new form to an ingrained and extensive piece of Americana.

Heading further east, you run into the Chenango County Historical Society (www.chenangohistorical.org). I have included this historical society as my partner in creating an engaging project for students in the classroom. In the summer of 1999, I led a series of social studies activities with rising 8th-grade students at a rural middle school in Chenango County, NY. One of our assignments involved researching the pioneer cemetery in the village. As the students were looking at gravestones, I had asked them to identify what major historical events the deceased could have lived through. After reviewing the burial ground, the students went into the village library (right next door) and looked for information about the people and the events. It was at the library that one young man started me on the trail of Charles Parsons, War of 1812 vet. The stone had no marker, nor were their indications that Mr. Parsons had served in the military. Using traditional research techniques, and the afternoons the summer session allowed me, I investigated. After four weeks, and the use of newspaper clippings, Chenango county records, and war records held in the County historical society, we as a class were able to confirm that Charles Parsons did serve in the War of 1812. This is a pivotal turning point experience for rural students who hated history to see how research can result in finding clues and discovering mysteries to solve.

Northeast of Norwich lies the former New York State Historical Association, now the Fennimore Art Museum (www.fenimoreartmuseum.org) in Cooperstown, NY. The archives and library at the former NYSHA are chocked full of information about state history, local and national history, which emerged in New York State. Unlike the New York City-based association, the Cooperstown archive has a treasure trove of artifacts, documents, and materials that local schools would want to use for their own history and their local town's history. One of my favorite findings among the collection was letters of sympathy written to the Lincoln family after the President's assassination. These documents demonstrate connections locally, at the state level to a national historic event. It also reminds us of the work that Carol Kammen of

Cornell University (Kammen, 2014) did on local history. Kammen describes the essential role local historians and history play in filling in details to major national trends and events. What is even better, however, is a reminder that local history can be told as an essential part of the narrative which historians wish to construct. It is important to remember the local history matters are closest to our students, especially those who are disenfranchised by the grand narrative containing no one who looks like them.

Our local libraries, local historical associations, and archives have a treasure trove of materials just waiting to be rediscovered by students. At an early age, children love museums and the discoveries which await. If we do not allow students to go behind the scenes, and get hands-on experience, then our curious children grow into adults who are incapable of valuing the past and listening to its voices.

The Museum of Art Gallery (mag.rochester.edu) in Rochester, part of the University of Rochester, has a fantastic artist program for students in its museum. It also contains sources which would really help implement the Common Core into the classroom. Its materials and curatorial staff have done an amazing job telling the story of world history in an accessible way. The museum and its workshops and activities are designed to facilitate critical thinking, creativity, and engagement. These three areas most closely resemble what the Common Core asks for in its standards-based approach to education.

What collections for local history are present in your community? **#ThinkingAboutTeachingBook**

$\mathcal{M}$y home state of New York has many such examples of technological advances within its borders, from the Erie Canal (www.eriecanalway.org/ explore/plan-your-visit/category/historic-and-cultural-sites-and-museums) to the use of iron by the Burden Iron (www. hudsonmohawkgateway.org/BIWMWhatIsIt.html) works. The mighty Niagara is an example of the raw power that nature can offer to a civilization when it harasses the water for use in manufacturing. There is a massive amount of kinetic energy emerging from the power of the river as it passes over the falls. The power project in the Niagara region diverts a tiny fraction of the water from the river to turbines. So much cleaner energy could be made by using the water instead of coal or oil or other fossil fuels. The Cooperstown Museum does a great job of exploring a wide range of technology. The farmer's museum starts with early 1800s era farm technology and displays how those machines were in use. The museum also takes up how the transition between muscle power to internal combustion engines impacted the villages in the area. As crop yields rose, and transportation to market became powered, fewer people were needed on farms and moved to the cities seeking new work. These people moving to the cities became enmeshed into urbanization that dramatically impacted people, families, and communities. The societal impact of technology is clearly examined in the Brooklyn Tenement Museum. Imagine working in soot-covered city buildings instead of clean rural air. Imagine living in a building with no running water, almost 12 people to a single room? This is what many urban dwellers, both immigrant and migrant, faced as they entered New York City to work in the mechanical steel world. The human side of history is critical to understand in our explanation of the past. Several amazing native culture museums explore the worlds of indigenous people. In Cobleskill, the Iroquois Museum (www. iroquoismuseum.org) allows visitors to see the art, economy, politics, and families of our native forebears. Cooperstown has some living history longhouses, which give people a taste of the way natives lived before colonization. The museums across New York help us remember that not only are natives critical to the past but live in the present. Especially in our schools, it is critical to help students see the present in their cultural groups.

These museums are excellent partners for teachers who seek to have students see their textbooks come alive. Specifically, teaching about germs could involve a discussion of the smallpox virus (www.oldfortniagara.org) and its devastating effects on Native Communities in North America.

New York City is also blessed with the Cloister (www.metmuseum.org/visit/met-cloisters), a museum that examines the Middle Ages. Large metropolitan museums, such as this one, often do an excellent job covering the role diseases play in human history.

Outside of New York, I would strongly recommend traveling to the ROM (www.rom.on.ca/en). This Toronto-based facility houses many amazing collections on the history of humanity in a fantastic curated facility. Additionally, there are several museums and living history sites across the US. Many in fact have educational programs which classrooms really ought to use. As an educator, I always wished I had a bigger travel budget, and wanted to do a better job teaching my students about the past. With the internet, some travel can be eliminated, but you may wish to see if the organizations have grant money set aside to help get your students to their location.

I hope you enjoyed these thoughts and two resources: one on the cold, and another on germs and the technology we use daily. Now, I am going to go drink tea, eat chicken soup, and take some cold medicine for this acute viral nasopharyngitis (or common cold) I'm suffering from!

REFLECTION INTERLUDE

Take a moment and write about the best lesson you ever taught:

Take a moment and write about the worst lesson you ever taught:

Never have I ever...but now I want to!

So far, I have talked about myself. Usually, when I read a book, I want to write myself a note about my takeaways for the classroom. Use the rest of this page to write down one technique learned in this book that you want to try.

PART III

RURAL EDUCATION

A VOICE NO LONGER LOST IN THE WILDERNESS

Being a teacher is tough—being an educator in a disadvantaged location is an even more laborious task. While several texts and podcasts examine urban educators, I wanted to try and talk about rural education. The teachers working daily in rural schools face several issues, including poverty, community decline, and political apathy. Resources are scarce. Pay is often low, and opportunities for growth can be limited. BUT, rural educators often overcome difficult odds and enact amazing and awe-inspiring tasks! I hope that as you read this next section, you gain some understanding, or appreciation, or insight that will help you or your students.

31. SEPARATE BUT NOT EQUAL

The 1954 landmark Supreme Court decision Brown v. Board of Education reversed Plessy V. Ferguson. These two cases mark the bookends of the beginning and theoretical end of segregation by race in the United States. At that moment, the Supreme Court made an admission that segregation was wrong, and the Court needed to right this wrong. We should remember this fact not as political flip-flopping, but as rationed and reasoned debate.

There have been many injustices across time that need their "Brown" moment in the United States. Under Johnson's Great Society, the ESEA, or Elementary and Secondary Education Act of 1965, created the Title I funding to try to alleviate poverty for students who were falling behind their wealthy peers. As Sean Reardon of Stanford University has pointed out, we have a multitude of school districts where the rich are clustered with the wealthy, and the poor are left to look at the better systems across the tracks (Bischoff & Reardon, 2014). We have yet to meet the overall needs of our students in poor communities in the USA.

Having served the New York State Education Department Office of School Improvement for seven years, I saw firsthand schools that would have made urban reformer Jonathan Kozol (1991) scream at the injustices committed against children. Kozol has written several works showing the utter decay in many urban schools. His work is a must-read for people interested in school reform. The bathrooms didn't work; there was no hand soap. Teachers struggled with students who spoke another language fluently but were trying to learn English. I saw promising programs and promising young teachers cut because of budget difficulties. I saw educators struggling with the overwhelming mental and emotional needs of children who lived in war zones.

When Millikan V. Bradley was handed down, the court essentially said that *de facto* segregation *because of an invisible line* was perfectly OK.

Whoops. We didn't even make it past the 1970s.

There needs to be a change in education, and it needs to happen in rural and urban schools alike. The eminent geographer Mark Monmonier of Syracuse University covers these points in his works, which include *How to Lie with Maps* and *No Dig, No Fly, No Go* (2010). Lines are powerful, especially on maps. Just ask the Native Americans, Africans,

South Asians, and East Asians. Rusk's (1995) work, *Cities without Suburbs,* describes what happened to northern cities when the suburban communities surrounding them became legal, separate entities. Resources were no longer shared; instead, wealth fled to the farmland developed into McMansions as the inner core decayed. Suburbs were developed with substantial governmental aid in the form of utility subsidies and mortgage and tax breaks for homeowners outside of cities.

In rural communities, we haven't had our day in court to force increased resources to rural schools. In my first year of teaching, I was asked to teach 7th, 9th, 11th, and economics in a small school of 275 students in grades K-12 school. My Global Studies textbooks were paperback, and missing the covers and the first chapter or two. I had limited resources, so I begged a company to donate maps of the United States and the world, which they gave to the school.

We had wall maps (think: pre-computer or SMART Board days)!

I had students who told me that they could not go to college because of family poverty. I had students who had never been to a bigger city than Buffalo, NY.

In some rural communities across the US, the internet hasn't quite reached there yet. In rural Delaware County, NY, one school is so isolated that there is no cell phone coverage.

When I was teaching in my next job, I found myself wondering what would happen to our kids when they went away to college. Thankfully, many did alright. I count among our blessings a State Trooper, small business owner, doctor, lawyer, and certified massage therapist among the graduates.

One of the facts facing our rural schools is this: size does not, nor should not, equal dollars. Just as poverty takes more money to correct, rural poverty and rural isolation are difficult to correct. As we see after the 2016 election, the attention to rural areas and rural poverty requires teachers, scholars, students, and professionals to learn about and include rural areas, communities, and, most importantly, people in the solutions to overcome the local challenges of small size and small resources. Major US news outlets, including *The Atlantic*, *The New York Times*, and *Newsweek,* have all discussed the crisis, which is emerging in rural areas as people become mad about being overlooked. Cramer (2016), Wuthnow (2018), and Catte (2018) have all written book-length studies on how people in rural areas are angry, feel overlooked, and are sure that their way of life is in jeopardy. NPR and other news radio outlets have taken time out of their busy broadcasting schedule to examine politics, sociology, and economics in rural areas. Our country has an under-resourced part of its very core—the rural regions along the Appalachians and the Great Plains and the Deep South, which have a simple demand: please respect us.

The sentiment of how the locals are at fault for the desperate state of their community needs to change. Since the late 1800s, several outside authors have perceived the rural world as "backward." This deficit model of writing fails to remember that rural areas were the cornerstone of several inventions. Central New York played a pivotal role in the development of Science Technology Engineering and Math (STEM) in the U.S. For example, the Norwich Aspirin Company founded and marketed several health care products used in pain relief and first aid. These included Unguentine, Pepto Bismol, and aspirin tablets. Then it was bought out by the Proctor and Gamble multinationals, and poof! There went the good jobs.

Charles Dudley, a famous chemist, lived in Oxford, NY. He developed many steel-related processes for the railroad companies he worked for. His research led to changes in how railroads used fuel, steel, and other chemical and industrial based activities. To the south, Sidney, NY, hosted many air- and space-related companies. In the Bendex plant, some of the original flight gyroscopes were invented and manufactured. If you look at David Richard's doctoral thesis, you can see how the manufacturing community in the area grew and developed, especially around World War II. STEM can exist in rural areas, but we as a society must give them money, opportunity, and a chance.

Look no further than Leanne Avery and her work on Place-Based Pedagogy. Change the narrative from local rural schools are deficient to local rural schools are innovative places. I, for one, would feel that any research conducted by rural students into STEM fields, or skilled tech jobs, is an appropriate endeavor for teachers who are searching for an answer on how to motivate their students.

Let's take All-Terrain Vehicles (ATVs) for a moment as a lesson stop. An ATV, as the recreational vehicles are known colloquially, are magnets for youth in rural areas to talk about, obsess over, and ride. An ATV is a great point to stop and discuss a wide range of historical, scientific, and technological progress with your students. There are several implications, so let's spend some time reviewing them:

ATVs were initially designed as a way for farmers to move about their fields easily without the encumbrances of large farm vehicles. The tool became popular with hunters and outdoorsmen to use as a way to transport supplies into the woods for camping and to transport hunting gains out to the roadways. The ATV was designed as a way to allow people to ride in areas that are not suitable for golf carts, which require smooth, level ground. The ATV also met a need for a broader base to provide greater transportation and hauling abilities than a dirt bike could provide.

ATVs evolved and were designed with internal combustion engines, extensively over-engineered drive trains, and rugged construction to withstand the abuse of working life. The ATVs were assembled in such a way that the "everyman" could repair the equipment out in a field, without the need for extensive tools. ATVs became popular recreational tools for people to begin to race, take to obstacle courses, and drive recreationally on weekends. For many children in rural areas, the ATV became the way that legally they could drive a vehicle for the first time and support the farm or hunting or resource extraction activities of their families.

The ATV has a history. The mechanical parts of an ATV are intricate. Communities are in conflict in how ATV usage is defined by law and valued by local residents and tourists. So many different areas to explore—a perfect example of a place-based pedagogy to inspire and intrigue students!

What are local areas of interest you would like to explore with your students? **#ThinkingAboutTeachingBook**

32. AMAZING RURAL EDUCATION PRACTICES

*S*ome amazing rural educational practices happen daily in the American system. Why don't more people know about the amazing happenings at our smallest schools? Mostly, our press is devoted to what is going wrong in schools. It is easier to find problems in the schools than to see what is right. Some of our hardest-working teachers live and ply their trade in public, small, rural communities. Day in and day out, these superheroes of the classroom devise lesson plans that are engaging, creative, and thought-provoking. These lessons help students study the core areas of English language arts, social studies, math, science, physical education, art, world language, and technology. So, what are these engaging practices?

Best Practice One: Cross-Curricular Connections

Our first practice is the integration of curriculum. Teachers from different grade levels and different content traditions work together daily to ensure the students get to learn beyond the disciplines and into the integrated learning experiences. When I was working at Sidney CSD, an ELA teacher and I worked together to ensure that our students in the ninth and tenth grades were seeing the two curricula working in harmony. Why did we do this? Because we shared the same students.

The kids saw me in first period and saw her second period. If we had expanded the efforts to science and art and music as well, the students could have experienced a schedule that would have looked like this:

1st Period: Social Studies — History and culture of the Middle East
2nd Period: ELA — Literature of the Middle East
3rd Period: Earth Science — Geological formation of oil and water bodies in the Middle East
4th Period: Music or art of the Middle East
5th Period: Foods from a Middle Eastern menu
6th Period: Math using Middle Eastern concepts (Algebra, zero theory)
7th Period: Physical Education—athletic events invented in the Middle East

8th Period: Technology—Saltwater desalination in the Middle East

9th Period: Elective

The integration discussed here is only one example of how a small school could invite cross-curricular connections and help students see a place from many different angles.

Best Practice Two: Knowing Your Students

Many small rural schools take Wong and Wong's *First Days of School* (2009) advice to heart: greet each of your students by name and know something they are interested in. When I taught at Little Valley CSD, we had small classes, and we knew each student's name. We knew their families. We knew their hopes, dreams, and greatest fears. One student wanted to go to Fredonia, my alma mater. We worked hard as a school to try and get that student to open house day, and she would have made a great Fredonia student.

We also knew how hard it was for students to live in the fishbowl of the community. They were the 250 students who were enrolled in the district grades K-12. On Saturday, we supported the sports team, and we went to the play. We attended graduation.

Did we do this because it was in our contract? No.

We went as a faculty because the students were ours. The students and their parents were our neighbors. Hope Casto

(2016), a faculty member at Skidmore College, wrote a fascinating piece on parent involvement in a semi-rural community. The paper has some excellent insights into the difficulties administrators have in balancing parent involvement and running their schools. Dr. Hal Lawson, a professor at SUNY Albany, in his School and Community Relations class, reminds pre-certification administrators to not do everything alone—including working with parents and community members. Rural schoolteachers, help make sure that parents and community members feel welcome in the school.

Best Practice 3: STEM in the Community

When I was teaching at Sidney, three teachers won a grant to monitor the Susquehanna River from its source in Cooperstown, NY, to the Pennsylvania Border. Our students measured flow, quality, and a variety of hydrological and meteorological characteristics for one of the greatest water systems east of the Mississippi. This project took students into the field to conduct the monitoring activities and the write-ups for the National Oceanic Atmospheric Administration and other weather-related groups. The students would look at the level of pollution in the river. They also kept track of how dirty the water was and at what points it cleared up. The Sidney students who act as Susquehanna River monitors in their class, as well as the members of the US geological survey, are all interested in water levels—from the depth of the river to the levels of pollution and contamination. This activity helps students see value in the work they do, especially considering the "Sus" is connected all the way to the Chesapeake and is one of the original reasons why the village was settled.

Challenge

- Examine the #RuralEdChat on Twitter for more information. RuralEdChat is the international network of scholars and practitioners who communicate via the platform to exchange ideas, lesson plans, and research ideas.
- Find out what the NYS Center for Rural Schools is up to at Cornell University. They provide data, research, professional development, and public engagement to help rural schools throughout New York.

THESE ARE ALL GREAT PLACES FOR RESEARCH ON RURAL education and for the work in which we invest in our students daily!

33. RURAL RESEARCH

*T*oday I was looking at my draft dissertation researching rural areas, and I was thinking about the times I spent working with my students in one of my former schools. These students had lived their entire careers in one school, grades K-12. This school no longer officially exists.

From the minute they entered kindergarten until they graduated, the students were surrounded by friendly faces who greeted them each day. From the bus drivers to the cafeteria staff to the teachers, the principal, and superintendent, everyone knew each other. Mara Tieken, in her book *Why Rural School Matters* (2014), talks about the school as the center of the community. She explores two districts in Arkansas that are subjected to consolidation and state take over. A key point in her phenomenal text is the lengths the schools go to do right by their students.

As an outsider who became part of the inside, I found the rural communities to be places of unique cohesiveness. The formation of the community through the shared school experience is something which Peshkin (1978), DeYoung (1995), Theobald (1997), and Schafft (2006) have all written about to a greater or lesser extent. While thinking about how the rural became part of me, I wonder how my research can help rural communities survive and thrive.

I feel that in education, a policy shift needs to happen where we see more regional specialized schools like Tech Valley. Tech Valley is a hands-on learning environment in the Capital District of New York state. It is a collaborative endeavor between Our intermediary Board of Cooperative Educational Services (BOCES) to give students a chance to go in-depth into project-based learning on the campus of State University of New York Nano. If each BOCES area could specialize in one or two types of 21st-century prep programs, New York could see a renaissance in economics and academics. Each of our regions is specialized and has offerings that our students could explore in-depth. Regional re-investment is critical for helping smaller areas flourish. Who wouldn't want to learn conservation in the Adirondacks aside Blue Mountain Lake? What student couldn't enjoy learning large equipment repair in the St. Lawrence Seaway?

I propose that each BOCES explores not a professional-Tech school, but a specialty based upon the resources of its area. Back in my little school, which no longer exists, it would be amazing to have a geosciences-based school. The area was originally one of the more petroleum-rich regions. As we move away from fossil fuels, we still need petrol for chemicals. The Geosciences program at the BOCES would allow students to research and earn an associate's degree in geosciences from the community college and their high school diploma while launching their learning into a hard science based on a community need.

It's time to use our rural resources correctly. This may include allowing students the opportunity to transfer to a rural school for safety and program magnets. If most of our colleges are in rural areas, why can't our advanced high schools be centered around those schools?

Since the 2016 election, a whole slew of articles from all over the world has emerged about what to do with the rural areas of different countries. For many of the writers of these articles, and the book authors as well, some have entirely ignored the rural areas' fears. I use the word fear because it is true…fear is real. Fear exists. Change is driven by a need to move beyond what is, but change is a cause of fear. What is known is comfortable. Even in the most disastrous situations, an outsider who has become an insider will defend the status quo, because the reality becomes part and parcel of their self-identification. In other words, the catastrophe, here long before me, is now mine, because I didn't change it. Rural areas are seeking to alter some changes which have created devastation within their very core existence.

First, in this changing world, their students are suffering in competition against Artificial Intelligence (AI). Yes, you read that correctly. AI or machines are now evolving beyond rote work, which drove hands-on labor out of the economy and now is beginning to focus on though based work. In the past, competition was measured against your neighbor or someone in the next village over. Then gradually, the competition moved regionally, then statewide, then nationally, and finally in the flattened global world, where information and technology and communication travel almost instantly across oceans (Friedman, 2005). As I sit here and write this work, students two buildings over are researching AI. They want to make machine learning and human learning seamless.

Second, our rural areas are facing a massive loss in population. While it can be said that human migration has always been rural to urban, there has not been this level of rural to urban flight since the first industrial revolution in the 1700s and 1800s. Theobald (1997), in *Teaching the Commons,* tracks this flight as a breakdown of not only the rural areas, but of the social structures of urban areas as well. As people move away from communities where every person is known to each other, anonymity develops. In many urban areas, residents become numbers, statistics, and lose their connections, which build the strength of a small community/ neighborhood. Residents are more concerned about being left alone than the block. I do my thing, and everyone else does theirs, but we do not interact or get to know each other.

Third, the poverty levels in rural areas are becoming overwhelming. Urban areas are hard hit with poverty as well, but those spaces have mass numbers and infrastructure to deal with some of the negative impacts of poverty, which rural areas suffer from unbroken. The poverty in these regions is due to industrial flight, decreased mid-skill positions in resource extraction, and increased reliance on poor for service economy labor, which drives wages down.

Fourth, opioid addiction is running unabated in some of these areas across the US. A Rockefeller Institute (Malatras, 2017) study concluded that rural areas are seeing more per capita impact of the opioid addiction than their suburban or urban counterparts, with fewer resources and infrastructure to make do. Families are breaking apart; police and medical facilities are overwhelmed. Rural areas are bearing the brunt of the opioid crisis, and it is affecting the schools. As this public health emergency evolves, educators must take heed of how best to help students impacted in their classroom by these emergencies in the community.

With these significant obstacles facing rural areas, the school systems cannot continue with the status quo. The systems need to change, and quickly, to ensure the rural parts of the country do not die.

What are some problems of practice facing your local community? **#ThinkingAboutTeachingBook**

34. REFLECTING ON RURAL

After reading White and Corbett's (2014) essays on rural education and doing research in rural settings, I was thinking back to my first teaching assignment. I had just graduated from college with a BA in social studies for grades 7-12 and history education from Fredonia (Go Blue Devils!). I wanted so badly to teach social studies. I had grown up in a suburban environment near Buffalo, NY. As the summer drifted into fall, panic began to set in as no job was on the horizon. Miller (2012) found that many teachers would like to remain close to home. I was one of those teachers, yet a job offer was near. In late August, I was given an excellent opportunity to join the rural students, staff, teachers, and community in a small district that no longer exists.

That year, I became part of the community of a K-12 school, with only 250 students, teaching economics in grades

7, 9, 11, and 12. I shopped in the local market, ate lunch in the local diner (when I didn't eat cafeteria food), and went home 40 miles away to spend time with my family. What I realized more than anything else is that every child in a community that small is valued. All the teachers know the family and their students. When one of the seniors dropped out, it impacted everyone.

Under NCLB, the accountability sting was never more hurtful than the personal feelings of dread, that you had let a family down. The system is not a *system* in a small, rural community—it is an extended family. I was struck again and had flashbacks to my days at my first teaching job when I read Mara Tieken's (2014) work *Why Rural Schools Matter*. Her work in the two school districts in Arkansas reminded me of my time in my small rural village. The work has become central as I write my dissertation on rural school reorganization.

A second, greater reason caused me to think about my first position at that small rural school, though. As I write this paragraph, I ran into a success story from my first year of teaching. One of my students had a tough go of it in high school. She became pregnant in her sophomore year. She kept the baby and married the father. She graduated from high school, finished a college education, and is now looking to become an administrator after a successful start to an amazing teaching career. As the final three interviews were conducted by the district, this former student of mine was a finalist for the

Director position that I, too, was a candidate to assume. I remember years ago, as the seniors were graduating from my small little district of 245 students, grades K-12, this young scholar went into teaching and was competing sixteen years later for a Director Position. In a way, this at-risk student had overcome the odds and became (and continues to be) successful.

For all of the challenges of small, rural schools, there is hope and promise. Education needs to capture the best of curriculum offerings in large suburban schools, with the closeness and personal connections of the littlest rural districts. As I advance in my dissertation journey, from the literature review to the methods section, to findings and conclusions, I hope I may add a small bit of knowledge to the research on rural education. Having taught in a rural area, lived in two rural areas, and served rural students while at the state, I am invested in rural education.

35. A REFLECTION ON "HILLBILLY ELEGY"

S o I am, at heart, a rural educator. But I have served in rural schools, urban schools, government agencies tasked with working in schools, and higher education. I am in my 40s, having spent almost seven years in rural schools, and two years in an urban school (directly) with almost seven years tangentially. I have been in higher education for nearly four years. Middle age is causing me to reflect an awful lot on my experiences and, as the sociologists like to say, privileges. I want to lay that out up front: I am privileged. My family was nuclear, we had many hard-working aunts and uncles who surrounded us. I knew both sets of grandparents. We had friends of the family who were close and were surrogate aunts and uncles. My parents worked very hard for stability, and when we traveled, educational experiences were the heart of the matter for our visits. Yet there were rough times too: Dad getting structurally unemployed (laid-off) by ConRail as it imploded. Losing Adam, my baby brother, who died due to birth defects. The family moving away from our nuclear support to Gloversville. The money that never seemed to be enough, but always was so that we had food, shelter, clothes, and experiences to museums.

Reading JD Vance's (2016) book *Hillbilly Elegy*, I alternated between understanding and amazement. I recoiled at some of his thoughts and supported others. I really think his text needs to be read in tandem with Kathy Cramer's (2016) work on the rise of discontent among the rural communities. It's an excellent book for one perspective on rural, rural poor, and rural white poor in difficult family situations. His efforts strive to give voice to a group that has been voiceless. It is a vivid retelling of his experiences from when he was young to his graduation from Law School. Vance uses the term Hillbilly to describe his family and their actions. Through this lens, the tale is told of life that moves from one crisis to another and then through redemption at the feet of his grandparents, his older sister, and the US Marine Corps.

I want to stop here and give thanks and praise to the US military for their efforts at raising "thrown away" children in the U.S. Quite often a story about how service in one branch or another has turned someone's life around by instilling a sense of order and discipline which was lacking.

JD's family experienced many issues, ranging from drug and alcohol problems, the de-industrialization of the Midwest, instability in the nuclear family, and the disinvestment of public education during K-12. His characterization of living in a Rust Belt City is more accurate than the rural connotation the title and many publicists have given the general public. I argue that reading this book, JD has given voice to a disenfranchised group of people in the inner city and small peripheral cities. As I was reading the text, I thought about Lois Weis's work *Working Class without Work* and Willis' *Learning to Labor*. Both examine the plight of large, urban city working class. Vance's work adds to the narrative for smaller and mid-sized cities. I would like to add that *Worked Over* by Doukas helps tell the tale of the Mohawk River Valley. To truly understand rural America, you really cannot equate one area with any other area. Each town, village, hamlet, crossing is unique in its own, individual, separate ways. Yes, common trends do exist, but rural cannot be grouped together, just like urban should not be combined into a monolith.

While JD's grandmother plays an exceptional role in the book until he loses her to death, he hints very gently about the lessons that he learned from her. This work is indeed his homage to her, and to the loving care which she provided. I wished he would have explored his sister's influence in more detail. She seemed to have done yeoman's work in protecting him from the extremes which his family overcame. While he is the central storyteller in the book, I believe that the text should be examined by feminist scholars for the way in which women influence life in different economic strata in the U.S.

The glass ceiling is a terrible wrong committed by power in society, but I think a recognition of the rock-solid foundation that women provide to many needs greater attention. If not, how many more families would fall ever further into the morass?

Vance's book raises a series of policy questions that need to be addressed: How do we get the Harvards, Yales, and Stanfords to do a better job reaching non-affluent applicants? Can the United States Education System examine itself beyond year-to-year testing and see how well schools provide movement into each child's own unique career pathway? Would a systematic health care policy that universally protected mental health, dental health, vision, and physical health reduce the number of school and family-related issues? Should the US government's next major infrastructure investment be in creating safe lead-free and mold-free housing in cities, suburbs, and rural areas? How can we better leverage the military's guidance system to help disaffected youth?

While we have programs like Troops to Teachers, we may need to deploy more service members into areas most affected by malaise. Not as an occupying force, but as mentors in communities where they are not found, or in short supply. Our military has been tasked with fighting terrorists abroad. There is a much greater need at home: fight the drug gangs, and fight the social anomie which has emerged in urban and rural areas from job losses and societal breakdowns.

Harsh words emerge within the text, and they can grate on

people who have never experienced the bias and the different norms that JD experienced. The question becomes how to stop the characterizations and the lack of tolerance and understanding, which Vance brings up in his memoir. It is a question that is unanswered in the book, and in many ways undecided by the academy.

JD Vance's work *Hillbilly Elegy* allows a peek into the mind of the white working class. A memoir with compelling experiences and moments of pain which come across to the reader in an easily accessible text, it should be an assigned course reader in a sociology and policy class at the graduate level.

How can educators advocate for equity for all students, especially those from rural areas?

#ThinkingAboutTeachingBook

36. THE ADVENTURES OF TEACHING SUMMER SCHOOL

I taught summer school for three summers in Sidney. The first year, I worked with seventh graders who were at risk of not becoming eighth graders. My next two years were teaching ninth grade for the regional summer school. First and most obviously, I needed the money. It was nice to have the added income of summer school employment when in the early stages of my career. It was also nice to experiment and change up instructions once in a while.

You need to understand a small point about summer school: it occurs in old brick buildings that are hot. No air conditioning. It's really muggy in those valleys during the summer. No one in the class wants to be there. The students want to be anywhere else. They would much rather be outside, or now, on a video game.

Additionally, many teachers don't want to be there—they

need the money. I wanted to be at this summer school for 7th graders. We created an interactive team approach with myself and an ELA teacher working on the Civil War as our theme. The students choose their own books at a Barnes and Noble Bookstore—not the library. We then took the students to the Pioneer Cemetery by the town library, where they spent the day looking for the founders of the village. They then created a timeline of events during the lifetimes of the pioneers. We then had the students mesh their learnings about the pioneers and the books that they selected from the bookseller, and had them complete a WebQuest on the internet on interesting events that they wanted to learn about.

It was structured with an element of choosing your own adventure. The group of 10 students, many of whom did not learn skills that school year, actually enjoyed the time we spent together examining a cascade of knowledge about their hometown and how it related to mid-1800s America.

At my other two summer school events, the students really did not want to be there. Ninth grade global was so dull to the students the first time. Many did not like the group activities I planned. The administrator hated anything that wasn't "traditional" and always indicated the need to "pound the facts until their ears bleed." More often than not, the ninth graders didn't see how the world of the ancients connected with their daily lives. I tried to interweave stories and little known facts, but quite often, the summer of their discontent caught up with them. For some students, they had passed the course but were absent too much from the regular year and had to attend summer school to make up seat time. This, to me, is so backward. Why would a school do that to students? I thought education had a goal of ensuring students demonstrated what they learned and then went to master the next skill. Not so much. The schools wanted seat time. The other huge issue I had with summer school was how downright crass some of the recommending teachers were towards the kids. Intentionally failing borderline kids because the teacher wanted to punish the kids for the summer. A last "I have power over you" moment.

School year learning is difficult enough when everyone is engaged. It is five times more difficult when no one is engaged.

What are some of your best strategies for engagement?
#ThinkingAboutTeachingBook

PART IV

THE CONCLUSION

By this point in the book, I hope I have not left you wondering why I tell my stories. My journey along a few pathways begins in Buffalo, NY, and ends (so far in Albany, NY). Instead of heading west for adventure and success, I headed east, with many detours in between. In this last section, I tell the tale of why I left a noble profession and moved on to a different world, higher education. I thought that my move was for selfish reasons, but in reality, I made a move to help change lives, just in a different venue.

Every educator will face challenges. Some, like me, will leave. Others will stay. No one is surrendering. Instead, you are finding the best possible fit for your skillset and your talent in this world. There is no shame in being a teacher. It is one of the highest callings a person can undertake—to serve and to mold EVERY future citizen of their nation and world.

There is no shame in leaving. The profession has been evolving from an exhausting but rewarding profession to a challenging undertaking. As one of my favorite school administrators said when demoted: There is no shame in my game. Other people have shame in THEIR game. I'm back where I belong—helping kids and teachers! I believe that as well—I am back, helping kids and their teachers!

37. WHY I LEFT TEACHING

*a*t what point in time do you give up? When does your identity, as defined by your occupation, become untenable? When, personally, do you say enough? For me, was it the daily grind of lesson planning, assessment creating, standards aligning? Or could it have been the accumulation of my beginning medical conditions of diabetes and sleep apnea? Maybe it was because I created too many pains in the backside for my boss, who wanted to be a superintendent when he grew up. Perhaps it was the kids in class who could see my heart wasn't in teaching at that moment due to the personal crisis of a divorce. It could have been trauma from the year before when one of our graduates was killed in Iraq, the parent of a student died in an auto accident, and then one of my former 10th graders took her life.

School doesn't prepare you for these disasters. There is no research really on how to help teachers leave. You get tossed personally, especially when the non-tenured reviews begin to indicate that your teaching is sucking. From the beginning of my time, my evaluations had been phenomenal. Exceeds standards! Then it all came crashing down. It got to a point where I was emotionally and mentally done.

I HAD ONE ALLY, AND SHE, TO THIS DAY, STAYS IN TOUCH WITH me. I miss seeing her and talking with her. More importantly, I miss how she advocated for students with special needs. One time, in my class, some students and parents complained about the so-called "preferential treatment" given to students who received special services. My co-teacher did a great thing, though. She educated them. She showed them what it was like to suffer from dyslexia. She showed them what it was like to have fine motor issues. She educated them on how to be better humans. She did the right thing. Thank you, Mrs. H!

I left teaching because, above all, I was disappointed in myself. I could not provide the necessary level of excellence I had given before. Mentally and physically, I was broken and spent. I made it from 1998-2004 teaching in schools. I became a statistic, a casualty of a flawed mentoring system, my own ego, and the forces which are chewing up educators and spitting them out.

What are some things schools and districts can do to retain educators in our field? **#ThinkingAboutTeachingBook**

38. SO...HOW DID WE GET HERE?

*S*ince 1983's *A Nation at Risk* (Gardner), public perception of teaching has changed. Teachers were once a respected profession. Now we are challenged at every turn. No longer are "feelings" and "gut instincts" good enough —now teachers need to deliver data-driven instruction in a reflective classroom. As a teaching profession, politicians, business leaders, and parents question our knowledge, skills, and abilities. We no longer have the ability as a profession to use our knowledge and expertise to teach students entrusted with our care. We look over our collective shoulders as administrators enter classrooms with rubrics, assessments, and mandates from the government to do better. *Do more with less* in our classrooms, our profession, and with our students is the new mantra in schools. Administration tells us: remember to differentiate instruction, use scientifically-based research, and engage students in their own learning.

For 20 years, education has changed amid reforms. The evolution of education tells how politicians lost faith in educators and demanded metrics to know students learned in the classroom. Rhetoric emerged, promoting 21st-century college and career-ready skills. Students need to do STEM and oppose cyberbullying, all the while scoring well on exams. New York State offers end of course exams, or Regents Exams, and has done so since the 1890s (Beadie, 1999). For several years, these exams were entry-level tests to gain admission to colleges in the United States. Reform movements swept the country. End-of-course exams became the way to "ensure" that children learn. Teachers and administrators suddenly became obsessed with number scores on tests—not the growth and learning in a classroom.

While the reform movement's critics call foul, some good did emerge from the depths of these conversations. Since before the Civil War, White and underrepresented populations were served by totally different school systems. In the south, White children attended high-quality schools, while state laws forbade people to teach Black children and adults how to read. The Jim Crow era, after the Civil War, continued this separation by race, and the attendant deep institutional racism that went with this. Starting in the 1960s, integration became the law of the land after the Little Rock Nine enrolled in school. This followed the Supreme Court's ruling in Brown v. Board of Education that separate education was not equal education (Goyette, 2017). President Lyndon Johnson called for and received revolutionary reform legislation called the Elementary and Secondary Education Act (Goyette, 2017). This act directed federal funding into high-poverty schools, such as those in the Southern Tier and inner cities in New York State. Additional rules began to question why schools segregated disabled children from their peers, and laws such as the Americans with Disabilities Act and the Individuals with Disabilities in Education Act required schools to physically and programmatically change to accommodate all children (Goyette, 2017). Later, the court ruled that schools must host children who speak another language (Lau v. Nichols, 1974, as cited in Goyette, 2017). Recent reforms include allowing homeless children a safe place in their home school (McKinney-Vento Act, cited in Goyette, 2017). A lot of reform = a lot of change.

Also, the country has changed educational policy when stimulated under adverse circumstances, such as foreign conflict. During the Cold War, our race with the Soviet Union became a quest for science. Billions in federal aid flowed into schools and universities—all because we, as a nation, lived literally under a Russian satellite. The next major push came from the roaring Asian economies, specifically Japan. Following a massive rebuild from World War II, the island nation destroyed American industry as leaders in the durable goods world. Japanese cars and electronics became top of the line. The nation realized our students were not keeping up with other children on standardized exams. As Goyette (2017) shows, American students were doing poorly on Programme for International Student Assessment (PISA)—the international math assessments.

The United States likes to be successful in competition. We, as a nation, have always wanted to win at all costs. Americans like winning in the Olympics. We like winning at international test rankings. It is worth remembering that the US does not take kindly to competitors. As the 21st century matures, our primary competition on the world stage is China, the Red Dragon of old. One of our World War II allies, China, now competes with the US for hegemony, as Russia re-emerges, creating fear in generations who grew up diving under desks in the event a nuclear war started. What is more, terrorism and international anxiety create an "America-First" mentality just as economics, information, and culture spread ideas and artifacts across the world.

Reflection is a corkscrew that unstops a wine bottle of memory. To the user, a corkscrew is a tool. To the cork, it is an assault weapon. As you carve into the cork, the chef, sommelier, or wine consumer has no thought for the cork—it has completed its mission. The care and concern are for the wine. Will it be just right for cooking or consumption? Is the wine as good as I understand it to be, or is it not as advertised? I wish to explore with you in the following pages some of the richness teachers need to recapture in their reflections.

As students analyze documents for their meter and word choice, Robin Williams's character in *Dead Poets Society* (Weir, 1989) reminds me as an educator to ask critical questions. More importantly, help students find passion in the passionless. Do not allow critical thinking and rational examination to destroy wonder, excitement, and quality engagement.

I think very clearly about debates students engaged in during my Social Studies class. These rural youngsters brought to life very mature thinking when talking about slavery, crusades, genocides, and the Holocaust. Their horror at the sheer ethical absence present in the writings of Ida Tarbell's exposés stand in stark relief to the food safety recalls we endure in the 21st century.

Where have the ethics gone? Did conservative warnings come true? Did taking God out of the school destroy our nation?

My own thoughts on this subject helped me as I was reading a fantastic book on local control of public schools. Scribner (2016) describes the interplay between morality and schools as a way to advance agendas—limit public education to limit change in society. Or would Thomas Jefferson shake his head in disbelief, as the supposed program to educate the masses has failed, according to late-night pundits? Jefferson called for an educated citizenry to ensure the Republic would stand (Conant, 1962). As a former Social Studies teacher, I cringe when I hear people unable to create informed arguments about public policy.

Will we, as educators, stand this test of time? Will we overcome the metaphorical hemlock handed to us by the city, claiming we corrupt young minds? Education is a noble profession that historically received short shrift. Rousmaniere (2013) calls the hatred spoken about educators' work as "disabling the profession" (p. 90). Other educational historians and journalists call this war on teachers for what it is: jealousy for hard-won concessions, which community members working in factory and industry and service industry lost to corporate resource redistribution. (Weis, 2013).

Lois Weis (2013) examined local people's views towards teachers in the 1980s. She found many had pity on professionals who needed to take summer jobs waitressing or painting a house just to make ends meet. This pitying view has changed dramatically, as Cramer (2016) found in her study examining rural people's opinion of public employees. Now, many rural people believe that public employees are a burden on society. My own dissertation research has found rural community residents feel that teacher salaries are too high for the work which they undertake (Jakubowski, in press).

McHenry-Sorber & Schafft (2015), in a ground-breaking study that examined conflict in rural schools during teacher contract negotiations, found devastatingly negative attitudes towards teachers. One person quoted in the survey threatened educators: "make my day—shoot a teacher." (p.1). As children hear their elders denigrate the profession, and as politicians demand more, it is no wonder that 2017 saw SUNY Chancellor and New York State Commissioner of Education declare a teaching recruitment emergency (SUNY, 2016).

Is it any wonder that almost 50% of teachers leave the profession by year five? I am one such "leaver," as the New Teacher Project reports (Johnson, 2004). I left the profession in year five. I did it for personal and professional reasons. I had no agency. I had no support. I was exhausted and burnt-out from the daily classroom management battles and the incessant "growth feedback" administrators insisted on giving faculty.

Feeling like a failure, I wanted to understand why I left. Enrolling in the University at Buffalo's Teacher Mentoring program, I learned the structures and systems in place in schools often hasten teacher flight, not prevent it. Reading Johnson (2004) and other works on teacher mentoring, I now know, almost half a decade later, my parents were right: I lived to teach content and did not really understand how to help students master knowledge in my classroom. I had yet to understand truly about scaffolding a lesson. How does one tie current events into the past? Now I know.

I am especially indebted to the experiences from the State Education Department, and the learnings gathered from my administrative leadership program. As I was simultaneously learning content in classes, I was working with people in the midst of trying to reform schools. They were facing an immense challenge: try and help students without much hope. I learned from an exceptionally brilliant cohort of fellow graduate students that there is much more to life than being smart. You need to understand what the people are experiencing during reform.

Education and society have always changed rapidly. Archaeology shows us this. History reaffirms this. Journalism covers this fact daily. When I first started teaching, there were a limited number of computers being used in the school, let alone a classroom. Most work for research still required a trip to the library. That has changed. You can now go and visit ancient monuments on a web browser. You can video chat with someone a world away on a smartphone. You can text, Facebook message, or Skype with family members a state, country, or continent away. It is critical and essential that new teachers learn how to prepare students for the next significant wave beyond the information age. Controlling information is the key to education. Controlling the story, or "spin," is what will make or break civilization.

39. CONCLUDING THOUGHTS ON 20 YEARS IN EDUCATION

*I*n ninth grade, I wanted to make social studies more interesting. I felt that I could teach social studies better than the teacher in front of the room who made us color maps and copy down unending lines of text from the chalkboard. I now realize, after pedagogy classes, that boring teaching is most clearly associated with bad classroom management and poor content knowledge. Boring teaching is lazy. The simple sage on the stage model of teaching with worksheets is designed to pass the time. There is no interaction. There is no common learning. There is no community of practice. If a teacher is only surface-knowledgeable and does not truly understand their content, they cannot see the connections, see the unique stories, see the advanced possibilities of moving beyond the mundane into the magnificent!

I also understand that teaching is a tough job. It is not critical care but so necessary, and humanity does not give, in America, a recognition of how hard teaching can be. I had seen with my own eyes the Iowa Skills assessments, the first standardized tests when I was in fourth grade. This has progressed because of the faulty "Texas Miracle" to NCLB, and now ESSA. Standards, assessments, accountability. Yes, some teachers got away with murder. Others, dedicated and driven, have left the profession, retired on their own volition, or were forced to due to the train wreck of our national education endeavors.

I started to work in a poor area, where the students desperately wanted stability. They wanted teachers to stay. The school, at only 240 of them, was too small to make a go of it and has merged and since closed. The kids there faced some really tough obstacles: teen parenthood, drugs, poverty, lack of jobs, and no access to educational programming which suburban schools receive. Contrast this to a nearby suburban district, where there are four world language classes, six levels of math, four types of bands, a rock climbing wall, and a yoga studio. For lunch, you have three options: a salad bar, a pasta bar, and a sandwich bar. Ten miles up the road, students are receiving one slice of bologna, two slices of bread, one slice of processed cheese, a carton of chocolate milk, and an apple. Our students in urban environments face violence and poverty, teen pregnancy, and drugs as well. Some have never been to a movie theater. Our rural students may never have seen a bus. Our urban students may never have seen a cow, except as food on a bun.

Would I want to do it again? I am not sure. Some of my former students almost 15 years out have successful careers, which they give me a small amount of credit for helping them achieve. That makes me feel like I did something right. But I am still haunted by the ones I could not reach. Sammy,[1] who wanted to go to Fredonia, but never showed up the day we were supposed to take her. Sally, who took her own life. Jerry, who failed 7th grade for the second time. Tommy, who I tossed out of class because he misbehaved, and later found out his dad was stern towards him and yelled constantly, and I was the only adult who cared for his success. Julia, who started seeing a guy 10 years her elder when she was a junior. Her friends came to me, and the best thing I could tell them was to talk to the guidance counselor. I wish I had stood up to the cabal of teachers who ran the buildings, but I was young and scared of losing my job.

I wished I had made real changes when at the State. There were some small victories, but it wasn't enough. Too many kids in the school systems I reviewed are "Waiting for Superman" (Weber, 2010) when, in reality, the kryptonite is in the very foundations of their schools. Charter schools are only as good as the accountability system for them. Public schools are only as good as the humans in them. It is a draining profession, education. There is no Hogwarts. Dumbledore, as fantastic as he and professors are at that school, are fictional characters. The most common type of teachers I have met are closer to Miss Jean Brodie (Spark, 1961): teachers who teach but are not sure of their actual impact. Many do not realize that they have a real impact on students. We are all looking for something, a spark, a sign, a phrase, or a word to help motivate us. Teachers, take up that spark, challenge, word, phrase, or dramatic gesture—your students need you now, more than ever!

Go forth and do GREAT, AMAZING, AWESOME, and INSPIRING acts of heroics every day for a career!

*NAMES ARE CHANGED TO PROTECT THE INNOCENT, AND people with very good lawyers!

REFERENCES

Ahmed, B. (2011). Unpaid interns: Real-world work, or just free Labor? *National Public Radio.* downloaded: https://www.npr.org/2011/11/16/142224360/unpaid-interns-real-world-work-or-just-free-labor

Aidinopoulou, V., & Sampson, D. G. (2017). An action research study from implementing the flipped classroom model in primary school history teaching and learning. *Journal of Educational Technology & Society*, *20*(1), 237.

Alexander, K. L., Entwisle, D. R., & Olson, L. S. (2007). Summer learning and its implications: Insights from the Beginning School Study. *New Directions for Youth Development, 2007*(114), 11-32

Allen, R. F., Dawson, J. C., Glenn, M. F., Gordon, R. B., Killick, D. J., & Ward, R. W. (1990). An archeological survey of Bloomery Forges in the Adirondacks. *IA. The Journal of the Society for Industrial Archeology*, 3-20.

American Nurses Association. (2001). *Code of ethics for nurses with interpretive statements.* Downloaded: Nursesbooks.org.

Amin, R. (2019). Computer-based testing to resume in New York. *Chalkbeat.* Downloaded: https://www.chalkbeat.org/posts/ny/2019/04/03/questar-testing-glitches-state-assessments/

Bailyn, B. (2011). *Voyagers to the West: A passage in the peopling of America on the eve of the Revolution.* Vintage.

Bain, K. (2004). *What the best college teachers do.* Harvard University Press.

Batt, E. G. (2010). Cognitive coaching: A critical phase in professional development to implement sheltered instruction. *Teaching and Teacher Education, 26*(4), 997-1005.

Beadie, N. (1999). From student markets to credential markets: The creation of the Regents examination system in New York State, 1864–1890. *History of Education Quarterly, 39*(1), 1-30.

Benjamin, V. (2014). *The history of the Hudson River Valley.* Overview Press.

Bischoff, K., & Reardon, S. F. (2014). Residential segregation by income, 1970-2009. *Diversity and disparities: America enters a new century,* 208-233.

Blume, J. (1971) *Freckle juice.* New York: Dell

Blume, J. (1972). *Tales of a fourth grade nothing.* New York: Dell.

Blume, J. (1980). *Superfudge.* New York: Dell.

Boyd, D., Lankford, H., Loeb, S., & Wyckoff, J. (2005). Explaining the short careers of high-achieving teachers in schools with low-performing students. *American Economic Review, 95*(2), 166-171.

Brittan, C. D. (1991). *A bad spell in Yurt.* Riverside, NJ: Baen

Bui, Q. (2014). The most common jobs for the rich, middle class, and poor. *NPR. downloaded:*https://www.npr.org/sections/money/2014/10/16/356176018/the-most-popular-jobs-for-the-rich-middle-class-and-poor

Canterbury, D. (2014). *Bushcraft 101: A field guide to the art of wilderness survival.* Avon, MA: Adams Media.

Casto, H. G. (2016). " Just one more thing I have to do": School-community partnerships. *School Community Journal, 26*(1), 139-162.

Catte, E. (2018). *What you are getting wrong about Appalachia.* Cleveland, OH: Belt Publishing.

Chiang, H. S., Clark, M. A., & McConnell, S. (2017). Supplying disadvantaged schools with effective teachers: Experimental evidence on secondary math teachers from Teach for America. *Journal of Policy Analysis and Management, 36*(1), 97-125.

Clancy, T. (1985). *The hunt for red October.* New York: Berkley Books.

Cleary, B. (1965). *The mouse and the motorcycle.* New York: William Morrow.

Cleary, B. (1968). *Ramona the Pest.* New York: William Morrow.

Conant, J. B. (1962). *Thomas Jefferson and the development of American public education.* University of California Press.

Cramer, K. J. (2016). *The politics of resentment: Rural consciousness in Wisconsin and the rise of Scott Walker.* University of Chicago Press.

Crosby, A. W. (2003). *The Columbian Exchange: Biological and cultural consequences of 1492* (Vol. 2). Greenwood Publishing Group.

Danielson, C. (2011). *Enhancing professional practice: A framework for teaching.* ASCD.

Dewitt, P. (2016). Instead of Finland, we should be more like Massachusetts. *Edweek.* Downloaded: http://blogs.edweek.org/edweek/ finding_common_ground/ 2016/12/maybe_instead_of_finland_we_should_be _more_like_massachusetts.html

DeYoung, A. J. (1995). *The life and death of a rural American high school: Farewell, Little Kanawha.* Garland.

Diamond, J. M. (1998). *Guns, germs, and steel: a short history of everybody for the last 13,000 years.* Random House.

Diamond, N., John, D. S., Bennett, R., Lindgren, A., Errisson, K., Press, R., ... & Bécaud, G. (2005). *The jazz singer.* AEC.

Disney, W. (1941). *Dumbo.* United States: Walt Disney World Films.

Dixon, D. (1992). *The practical geologist: The introductory guide to the basics of Geology and to collecting and identifying rocks*. Simon and Schuster.

Dolin, J., Black, P., Harlen, W., & Tiberghien, A. (2018). Exploring relations between formative and summative assessment. In *Transforming Assessment* (pp. 53-80). Springer, Cham.

Doukas, D. (2003). *Worked over: The corporate sabotage of an American community*. Ithaca, NY: Cornell University Press.

Downs, A. (1995). *Corporate executions: The ugly truth about layoffs--how corporate greed is shattering lives, companies, and communities*. Amacom Books.

Duckworth, A. (2016). *Grit: The power of passion and perseverance*. New York, NY: Scribner.

Dunn, R. E. (2012). *The Adventures of Ibn Battuta: A Muslim traveler of the fourteenth century, With a new preface*. Univ of California Press.

Dweck, C. S. (2008). *Mindset: The new psychology of success*. Random House Digital, Inc.

Fagan, B. (2000). The little ice age. NY, NY: Basic Books.

Farrell, P. F. (1995). *Through the light hole: A saga of Adirondack mines & men*. North Country Bk Incorporated.

Fast, K., & Örnebring, H. (2017). Transmedia world-building: The Shadow (1931–present) and Transformers (1984–present). *International Journal of Cultural Studies, 20*(6), 636-652.

Fenstermacher, G. D., & Richardson, V. (2005). On making determinations of quality in teaching. *Teachers College Record, 107*(1), 186-21

Fisher, L. A. (2018). Learning to love Machiavelli: Best practices in teaching primary source documents to struggling secondary readers of world history.

Fisher & Frey (2014) Checking for understanding. Alexandria, VA: ASCD.

Fleming, A., Michaelson, R., Youssef, A., Holmes, O., Fonbuena, C., & Robertson, H. (2018) Heat: the next big inequality issue. *The Guardian.* retrieved: https://www.theguardian.com/cities/2018/aug/13/heat-next-big-inequality-issue-heatwaves-world

Florida, R. (2014) The rise of the creative class. New York, NY: Basic Books.

Friedman, T. L. (2005). *The world is flat: A brief history of the twenty-first century.* Macmillan.

Gardner, D. P. (1983). A nation at risk. *Washington, DC: The National Commission on Excellence in Education, US Department of Education.*

Green, D. P., & Gerber, A. S. (2015). *Get out the vote: How to increase voter turnout.* Brookings Institution Press.

Greenleaf, R. (1977). *Servant Leadership.* New York: Paulist Press.

Goyette, K. A. (2017). *Education in America.* University of California Press.

Hadden, R. L. (1999). *Reliving the Civil War: A reenactors handbook.* Stackpole Books.

Heiser, P. (2017). Teacher shortage? What teacher shortage? *New York State School Boards Association.* Latham, NY: NYSSBA. downloaded: https://www.nyssba.org/clientuploads/nyssba_pdf/teacher-shortage-report-05232017.pdf

Hess, F. M. (Ed.). (2005). *With the best of intentions: How philanthropy is reshaping K-12 education.* Harvard Education Press.

Higginbotham, E., & Weber, L. (1992). Moving up with kin and community: Upward social mobility for black and white women. *Gender & Society,* *6*(3), 416-440.35-42

Howe, D. & J. Howe. (1979) *Bunnicula.* New York: NY, Atheneum Books.

Hughes, J. & T. Jacobson. (1986). *Ferris Bueller's day off.* Paramount Pictures.

Hunter, M. (1985). What's wrong with Madeline Hunter? *Educational Leadership, 42*(5), 57-60.

Johansen, B. E., & Grinde, Jr, D. A. (1990). The debate regarding Native American precedents for democracy: A recent historiography. *American Indian Culture and Research Journal, 14*(1), 61-88.

Johnson, A. H., Andersen, S. B., & Siccama, T. G. (1994). Acid rain and soils of the Adirondacks. I. Changes in pH and available calcium, 1930–1984. *Canadian Journal of Forest Research, 24*(1), 39-45.

June, A. (2016) Emeritus Professors make a case for their campus to tap their talents. *The Chronicle of Higher Education. Downloaded from:* https://www.chronicle.com/article/Emeritus-Professors-Make-a/236693

Kammen, C. (2014). *On doing local history.* Rowman & Littlefield.

Kennedy, D. (1978). The structure of Blackstone's Commentaries. *Buff. L. Rev., 28,* 205

Kozol, J. (1991). *Savage inequality.* New York, N Y: Crown Publishers.

Lampert, J., Burnett, B., & Lebhers, S. (2016). 'More like the kids than the other teachers': One working-class pre-service Teacher's experiences in a middle-class profession. *Teaching and Teacher Education*, (58)

Lazarus, E. (2002). Emma Lazarus. *The New Colossus. Emma Lazarus: Selected Poems and Other Writings (2002) https://www.poetryfoundation.org/poems/46550/the-new-colossus*

Levy, P. A. (1996). Exemplars of taking liberties: The Iroquois influence thesis and the problem of evidence. *The William and Mary Quarterly*, *53*(3), 588-604.

Lewis, C, Harding, P. & Aston, M., edited by Taylor, T. *Time Team's Timechester* (Channel 4 Books, 2000).

Lough, N. (2016). The athletic trap: How college sports corrupted the academy by Howard L. Nixon, II. *The Review of Higher Education*, *40*(1), 154-157.

MacLeod, J. (2018). *Ain't no makin it: Aspirations and attainment in a low-income neighborhood.* Routledge.

Malatras, J. (2017). *The growing drug epidemic in New York.* Albany, NY: SUNY Rockefeller Institute of Government. Accessed: https://rockinst.org/issue-area/growing-drug-epidemic-new-york/

Manguel, A. (2009). *Homer's the Iliad and the Odyssey: A Biography.* Canongate US.

Marcus, A. S., Stoddard, J. D., & Woodward, W. W. (2017). *Teaching history with museums: Strategies for K-12 social studies.* Routledge.

McColl, A. (2005). Tough call: Is no child left behind constitutional? *Phi Delta Kappan, 86*(8), 604-610.

McDaniel, S., & Yarbrough, A. M. (2016). A literature review of after-school mentoring programs for children at risk. *Journal of At-Risk Issues, 19*(1), 1-9.

McHenry-Sorber, E. C. (2011). *Competing values, competing narratives: Rural education politics in dual arenas.* The Pennsylvania State University.

McHenry-Sorber, E., & Schafft, K. A. (2015). 'Make My Day, Shoot a Teacher': tactics of inclusion and exclusion, and the contestation of community in a rural school–community conflict. *International Journal of Inclusive Education, 19*(7), 733-747.

McMartin, B. (1992). *Hides, hemlocks, and Adirondack history: How the tanning industry influenced the region's growth.* North Country Books.

McMartin, B. (1994), "Introduction," in McMartin, B.; Long, J.M., *Celebrating the Constitutional Protection of the Forest Preserve: 1894-1994,* Silver Bay, New York: Symposium Celebrating the Constitutional Protection of the Forest Preserve, pp. 9–10).

Miller, L. C. (2012). Situating the rural teacher labor market in the broader context: A descriptive analysis of the market dynamics in New York State. *Journal of Research in Rural Education (Online), 27*(13), 1.

Molen, G. (2002) *Minority Report.* 20 Century Fox.

Monmonier, M. (2010). *No dig, no fly, no go: How maps restrict and control*. University of Chicago Press.

Monmonier, M. (2018). *How to lie with maps*. University of Chicago Press.

Moore Johnson, S., & The Project on the Next Generation of Teachers. (2004). Finders and keepers: Helping teachers survive and thrive in our schools. San Francisco: Jossey-Bass

National Governors Association Center for Best Practices & Council of Chief State School Officers. (2010). Common Core State Standards. Retrieved from: http://www.corestandards.org/

National Council for the Social Studies. (2014). *College, career, and civic life (C3) framework for social studies state standards: Guidance for enhancing the rigor of K-12 civics, economics, geography, and history*. National Council for the Social Studies.

Nemecek, L. (2003). *The Star Trek: The next generation companion: Revised Edition*. Simon and Schuster.

New York State Constitution (1895). Article XIV. downloaded: https://www.dec.ny.gov/lands/55849.html

New York State United Teachers. (2012) Teacher Evaluation Rubric. downloaded: https://www.nysut.org/resources/all-listing/2012/september/nysut-teacher-practice-rubric

Nokes, J. (2013). *Building students' historical literacies: Learning to read and reason with historical texts and evidence*. Routledge.

Nye, J.L. (1990). *Mythology 101*. New York, NY: Warner.

Ocejo, R. E. (2017). *Masters of craft: Old jobs in the new urban economy*. Princeton University Press.

Optimus Prime https://en.wikipedia.org/wiki/Optimus_Prime

Outkast. (2003). *Hey Ya!* LaFace Arista Records.

PAD Cornell. (N. D.) Program in applied demographics- Cornell University. Downloaded: https://pad.human.cornell.edu/index.cfm

Perrin, A. (2018, March 23). Who doesn't read books in America? Retrieved from https://www.pewresearch.org/fact-tank/2018/03/23/who-doesnt-read-books-in-america/

Peshkin, A. (1978). *Growing up American; Schooling and the survival of community.* Chicago, IL: The University of Chicago Press.

Place, M. (1984) *The First Astrowitches.* New York, NY: Dodd, Mead, and Co.

Planel, P., & Stone, P. G. (Eds.). (2003). *The constructed past: experimental archaeology, education, and the public.* Routledge.

Porter, W. F. (2009). Wildlife exploitation in the Adirondacks. *The Great Experiment in Conservation: Voices from the Adirondack Park,* 87-95.

Power, D. (2014). Feedback is a gift. In *the Curve Ahead* (pp. 127-140). Palgrave Macmillan, New York.

Pryor, E. B. (1987). *Clara Barton: professional angel.* University of Pennsylvania Press.

Reardon, S. F. (2011). The widening academic achievement gap between the rich and the poor: New evidence and possible explanations. *Whither opportunity*, 91-116.

Reese, W. J. (2011). *America's public schools: From the common school to" No Child Left Behind."* Baltimore, MD: Johns Hopkins University Press.

Regan, M. (2016). What does voter turnout tell us about the 2016 election? *PBS Newshour.* Downloaded: https://www.pbs.org/newshour/politics/voter-turnout-2016-elections

Reynolds, M. F. (2011). *Doing history in the Adirondacks: Interpreting the park, the people, and the landscape.* Loyola University Chicago.

Richards, D. S. (2011). *A New Deal on the home front: Sidney, NY 1939–1945.* State University of New York at Binghamton.

Rosa, B. (2016). Civic learning for a civic society. *OnBoard Online* Downloaded: https://www.nyssba.org/news/2016/12/15/on-board-online-december-19-2016/civic-learning-for-a-civil-society/

Rousmaniere, K. (2013). Those who can't, teach: The disabling history of American educators. *History of Education Quarterly, 53*(1), 90-103.

Rowling, J. K. (2002). *Harry Potter and the sorcerer's stone*. Warner Bros.

Rudolph, R. J. (2019). Living history museum experience: The relationship among visitors, physical objects, digital technology, and human interpreters. Master of Arts Thesis. Muncie, IN: Ball State University. Accessed: https://cardinalscholar.bsu.edu/bitstream/handle/123456789/201715/RudolphR_2019-2_BODY.pdf?sequence=1&isAllowed=y.

Rusk, D. (1995). *Cities without Suburbs.* Washington, D.C.: Woodrow Wilson Center Press.

Savani, C. (2016) Are you being rigorous or intolerant? The Chronicle of Higher Education. https://www.chronicle.com/article/Are-You-Being-Rigorous-or-Just/236341

Schafft, K. A. (2006). Poverty, residential mobility, and student transiency within a rural New York school district. *Rural Sociology, 71*(2), 212-231.

Scribner, C. F. (2016). *The fight for local control: schools, suburbs, and American democracy.* Cornell University Press.

Secara, M. P. (2008). *A compendium of common knowledge, 1558-1603: Elizabethan commonplaces for writers, actors & re-enactors.* Popinjay Press.

Shenk, T. (2019). Already great. *Dissent, 66*(2), 7-12.

Shetterly, M. (2016). *Hidden figures.* New York, NY: William Morrow.

Sims, P. (2013). *Little bets: How breakthrough ideas emerge from small discoveries.* Simon and Schuster.

Sinek, S. (2014). *Leaders eat last: why some teams pull together, and others don't.* Penguin

Spark, M. (1961/1999). The prime of Miss Jean Brodie. New York, NY: Harper Perennial Press.

Straubhaar, R., & Gottfried, M. (2016). Who joins Teach for America and why? Insights into the "typical" recruit in an urban school district. *Education and Urban Society, 48*(7), 627-649.

SUNY Press Release (5/18/2016). Chancellor Zimpher, Commissioner Elia Announce Historic Partnership. Accessed: https://www.suny.edu/suny-news/press-releases/may-2016/5-18-16-teachny/

Sweney, M. (2006). American Idol outvotes the president. *The Guardian.* Downloaded: https://www.theguardian.com/media/2006/may/26/realitytv.usnews

Theobald, P. (1997). *Teaching the commons: Place, pride, and the renewal of community.* Routledge.

Tieken, M. C. (2014). *Why rural schools matter.* UNC Press Books.

Tuthill, K. (2003). John Snow and the Broad Street Pump. *Cricket 31*(3), 23-31. downloaded: https://www.ph.ucla.edu/epi/snow/snowcricketarticle.html

Vance, J. D. (2016). *Hillbilly elegy.* New York, NY: HarperCollins.

Vandsburger, E., Duncan-Daston, R., Akerson, E., & Dillon, T. (2010). The effects of poverty simulation, an experiential learning modality, on students' understanding of life in poverty. *Journal of Teaching in Social Work, 30*(3), 300-316.

Weber, K. (Ed.). (2010). *Waiting for"" SUPERMAN"": How we can save America's failing public schools.* PublicAffairs.

Weir, P. (1989). Dead Poets Society, film. *Touchstone Pictures, California.*

Weis, L. (2013). *Working-class without work: High school students in a de-industrializing economy.* Routledge.

White, S., & Corbett, M. (Eds.). (2014). *Doing educational research in rural settings: Methodological issues, international perspectives, and practical solutions.* Routledge.

Willis, P. (1978). *Learning to labour: How working-class kids get working-class jobs.* Routledge.

Winerip, M. (2011). Tiny town recruits students worldwide. *The New York Times.* Downloaded: https://www.nytimes.com/2011/06/13/nyregion/ tiny-newcomb-ny-recruits-students- worldwide.html

Wong, H. K., & Wong, R. T. (2009). *The first days of school: How to be an effective teacher.* Findaway World LLC.

Wuthnow, R. (2018). *The left behind: Decline and rage in rural America.* Princeton University Press.

Young, A. F. (1999). *The shoemaker and the tea party: Memory and the American Revolution.* Beacon Press.

Zuckerman, S. J. (2016). *Organizing for Collective Impact in a Rural Cradle-to-Career Network* (Doctoral dissertation, Ph. D. Thesis, University at Albany, Albany, NY, USA).

OTHER EDUMATCH TITLES

EduMatch Snapshot in Education (2016)
In this collaborative project, twenty educators located
throughout the United States share educational strategies that
have worked well for them, both with students and in their
professional practice.

The #EduMatch Teacher's Recipe Guide
Editors: Tammy Neil & Sarah Thomas
Dive in as fourteen international educators share their recipes
for success, both literally and metaphorically!

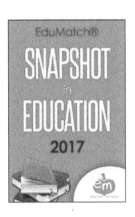

EduMatch Snapshot in Education (2017)
We're back! EduMatch proudly presents Snapshot in
Education (2017). In this two-volume collection, 32 educators
and one student share their tips for the classroom and
professional practice.

Journey to The "Y" in You by Dene Gainey
This book started as a series of separate writing pieces that were eventually woven together to form a fabric called The Y in You. The question is, "What's the 'why' in you?"

The Teacher's Journey by Brian Costello
Follow the Teacher's Journey with Brian as he weaves together the stories of seven incredible educators. Each step encourages educators at any level to reflect, grow, and connect.

The Fire Within

Compiled and edited by Mandy Froehlich

Adversity itself is not what defines us. It is how we react to that adversity and the choices we make that creates who we are and how we will persevere.

EduMagic by Sam Fecich

This book challenges the thought that "teaching" begins only after certification and college graduation. Instead, it describes how students in teacher preparation programs have value to offer their future colleagues, even as they are learning to be teachers!

Makers in Schools

Editors: Susan Brown & Barbara Liedahl

The maker mindset sets the stage for the Fourth Industrial Revolution, empowering educators to guide their students.

Divergent EDU by Mandy Froehlich

The concept of being innovative can be made to sound so simple. But what if the development of the innovative thinking isn't the only roadblock?

EduMatch Snapshot in Education (2018)
EduMatch® is back for our third annual Snapshot in
Education. Dive in as 21 educators share a snapshot of what
they learned, what they did, and how they grew in 2018.

Daddy's Favorites by Elissa Joy
Illustrated by Dionne Victoria
Five-year-old Jill wants to be the center of everyone's world.
But, her most favorite person in the world, without fail, is her
Daddy. But Daddy has to be Daddy, and most times that
means he has to be there when everyone needs him, especially
when her brother Danny needs him.

Level Up Leadership by Brian Kulak
Gaming has captivated its players for generations and cemented itself as a fundamental part of our culture. In order to reach the end of the game, they all need to level up.

DigCit Kids edited by Marialice Curran & Curran Dee
This book is a compilation of stories, starting with our own mother and son story, and shares examples from both parents and educators on how they embed digital citizenship at home and in the classroom.

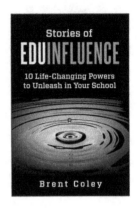

Stories of EduInfluence by Brent Coley

In Stories of EduInfluence, veteran educator Brent Coley shares stories from more than two decades in the classroom and front office.

The Edupreneur by Dr. Will

The Edupreneur is a 2019 documentary film that takes you on a journey into the successes and challenges of some of the most recognized names in K-12 education consulting.

In Other Words by Rachelle Dene Poth
In Other Words is a book full of inspirational and thought-provoking quotes that have pushed the author's thinking and inspired her.

To Whom it May Concern
Editors: Sarah-Jane Thomas, PhD & Nicol R. Howard, PhD
In To Whom it May Concern..., you will read a collaboration between two Master's in Education classes at two universities on opposite coasts of the United States.

One Drop of Kindness by Jeff Kubiak
This children's book, along with each of you, will change our world as we know it. It only takes One Drop of Kindness to fill a heart with love.

Differentiated Instruction in the Teaching Profession by Kristen Koppers
Differentiated Instruction in the Teaching Profession is an innovative way to use critical thinking skills to create strategies to help all students succeed. This book is for educators of all levels who want to take the next step into differentiating their instruction.

L.E.A.D. from Day One by Ryan McHale

L.E.A.D. from Day One is a go-to resource to help educators outline a future plan toward becoming a teacher leader. The purpose of this book is to help you see just how easily you can transform your entire mindset to become the leader your students need you to be.

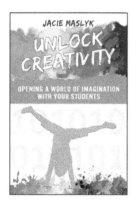

Unlock Creativity by Jacie Maslyk

Every classroom is filled with creative potential. Unlock Creativity will help you discover opportunities that will make every student see themselves as a creative thinker.

Make Waves! by Hal Roberts

In Make Waves! Hal discusses 15 attributes of a great leader. He shares his varied experience as a teacher, leader, a player in the N.F.L., and a plethora of research to take you on a journey to emerge as leader of significance.

21 Lessons of Tech Integration Coaching by Martine Brown

In 21 Lessons of Tech Integration Coaching, Martine Brown provides a practical guide about how to use your skills to support and transform schools.

Everyone Can Learn Math by Alice Aspinall
How do you approach a math problem that challenges you?
Do you keep trying until you reach a solution? Or are you like
Amy, who gets frustrated easily and gives up?

EduMagic Shine On by Sam Fecich, Katy Gibson, Hannah
Sansom, and Hannah Turk
EduMagic: A Guide for New Teachers picks up where
EduMagic: A Guide for Preservice Teachers leaves off. Dr.
Sam Fecich is back at the coffee shop and is now joined by
three former students-turned-friends. She is excited to
introduce you to these three young teachers: Katy Gibson,
Hannah Sansom, and Hannah Turk.

Unconventional by Rachelle Dene Poth

Unconventional will empower educators to take risks, explore new ideas and emerging technologies, and bring amazing changes to classrooms. Dive in to transform student learning and thrive in edu!

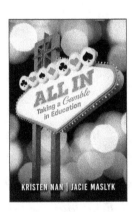

All In by Kristen Nan & Jacie Maslyk

Unlike Nevada's slogan of "what happens in Vegas, stays in Vegas," this book reminds us that what happens in the classroom, should never stay within the classroom!

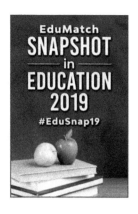

EduMatch Snapshot in Education 2019
EduMatch® is back for our fourth annual Snapshot in
Education. Dive in as an international crew of educators
share a snapshot of what they learned, what they did, and how
they grew in 2019. Topics include Social Emotional Learning,
identity, instructional tips, and much more!

Play? Yay! by BreAnn Fennell
Play? Yay! is a book my mom wrote for kids. I'm a toddler,
and I like to read. I sit and look at pictures or point to my
favorite pages. Do you like books like that? Then this book is
for you too! The best part about this book is that you can read
it with people like moms, dads, or grandparents. Get Play?
Yay! today for fun, rhymes, and the gift of imagination.

The EdCorps Classroom by Chris Aviles

Something happens when you launch an EdCorps in your classroom. An EdCorps, or Education Corporation, is what you get when you teach your curriculum through entrepreneurship. Any grade, any subject can harness the real, relevant learning that follows when you bring student-run entrepreneurship to your classroom. In this how-to guide, Chris Aviles tells you how he accidentally stumbled into the world of student-run businesses, and how you can use them to provide authentic learning to your students.

EduMatch Publishing

CPSIA information can be obtained
at www.ICGtesting.com
Printed in the USA
LVHW050017220722
723990LV00003B/604

9 781970 133226